PSYCHO CHICKEN
& OTHER FOOLISH TALES

Mike Girard

Sons of Liberty
Publishing

Nashua, New Hampshire

PSYCHO CHICKEN & OTHER FOOLISH TALES
Sons of Liberty Publishing, December 2010
Sons of Liberty Publishing, LLC
Nashua, NH 03062

PSYCHO CHICKEN & OTHER FOOLISH TALES
Copyright © 2010 Mike Girard
ISBN-10: 1453825614
ISBN-13: 9781453825617
Edited by Lloyd L. Corricelli
Cover Art by Don Mousseau
Digital Media Design - www.dmdgo.com
Proofed by Mary Davey Morley and Paula Ward Joyal

ACKNOWLEDGEMENTS

Mary Davey Morley, with her legal advice and keen editing.

Lisa Z, with her unending encouragement and friendship.

Of course my partners in crime, past and present; my Foolish band mates.

There were also the many people who helped me hunt down pictures; Steve Foote and Tom Reynolds found me some ancient Footestock photos and Jim Dort and Jeani Knowlton found a rare Gino shot. The great Boston rock photographer Ron Pownall took many shots of us in the eighties, some of which are in this book-including the cover shot of the First Annual Official Unofficial Fools Day album recording of a national broadcast from My Father's Place in Long Island.

The picture on the back cover of the book was taken by our own no. 7... Fred Mozdziez, the 7th best roadie we've ever had.

And finally, one night after a show in the fall of '09, a man came up to me and asked me why I'd stopped writing a monthly blog on my band's website. I said I didn't think anyone was reading it. He said "I was," and asked me if I ever thought of writing a book. I said yes and he handed me a card. A month later this book was begun, but it would never have happened without the help, guidance and encouragement of editor, publisher, and now friend Lloyd Corricelli.

The following story is mostly true part of the time, and partly true most of the time; but let's remember that some of these incidents happened many years ago and time can scramble the ingredients of a story. Comic artist Gahan Wilson once said, "I paint what I see." In my case. "I painted what I think I remember I saw."

Let the chips (and dips) fall where they may.

Mike Girard
October 2010

"…a group with balls, The Fools!"
Charles Laquidara
WBCN Radio
April Fool's Day 1979 live broadcast from
the Paradise Theater, Boston

To Ginny, my love, my friend, and my first line of defense, through most of this and more, and to my darling Sara, who is living her own story.

CHAPTER ONE

The Big Tex

"Not all those who wander are lost."
J.R.R. Tolkien

The year is 1981 and Ronald Reagan is the president. *Raiders of The Lost Ark* is the number one movie in the world and John Lennon's great posthumous album, *Double Fantasy*, tops the music charts. A brand new cable television station called Music Television (MTV) is in its first year and Germany is still divided by 'The Wall.' Common usage of the cell phone is still seventeen years away and no one knew what an MP3 was, let alone a compact disc. Computers still primarily involved men with thick glasses and pocket protectors punching holes in manila cards, and being online meant standing and waiting for something.

In spite of all this, or better yet at the moment, oblivious to this, two large campers are careening east across the Texas Panhandle, one of them billowing smoke. The campers contain a total of nine people, seven of which are horribly drunk, and in some cases, also stoned. Only the two drivers have refrained from joining the party. Driver number one is a German stage lighting designer of indeterminate gender named Fritz. Fritz is a perfect human specimen who doesn't drink because he feels alcohol makes people stupid. Tonight he is right.

Driving the other vehicle is a veteran rock 'n roll tour manager named Derek Dialdo who we'll call Dildo from now on. He's a Brit, and despite his well earned rep as a "bombs away" drinker, tonight he's not drinking for two reasons; neither of which has to do with responsible driving. Reason number one: he thinks the band he road manages has gotten wind of the fact that he reports back nightly to their New York management firm. And reason number two: he thinks the band is reporting back nightly on him to that same firm. In truth the band is well beyond both of these concerns.

They have spent a good part of the summer touring as the opening act to the most popular hard rock band in the nation, Van Halen, and have already played twenty shows in thirty one days and have traveled from Halifax, Nova Scotia to Inglewood, California. This is not this band's first major tour; for the last two years they've been crisscrossing North America and Europe playing with some of the world's great rock bands. Unfortunately for them though, this tour is different.

The band was warned from day one of the tour that few backup bands lasted more than a couple of shows with Van Halen. A full throttle rock event, Van Halen ruled eighties big arena rock, and yet they treated any applause awarded the opening act as a personal affront. Fuck you if our people liked you...as if it were all a testosterone fueled battle of the bands in some shithole L.A. bar on the Sunset Strip. The guys from Van Halen would name this tour by the acronym W.D.F.A. (WE DON'T FUCK AROUND). We had a different name for it; T.G.O.R. (THE GRIPES OF ROTH)

Who are we? We're a band called The Fools. Who am I? My name is Mike Girard, and I'm the singer in the band, and I'm also one of the guys in the camper that's billowing smoke. Okay, let's be clear, I'm not billowing smoke, the camper is. You may not have heard of us, but we've been around since New Year's Eve 1976, and through some act of fate, luck, or The Great Hairy Thunderer, we're still playing all these years later.

Over the years we've had a few almost hits, and in the seventies, eighties and nineties we either played with, or backed up, a large number of iconic rock bands. So what does it all mean? Who knows, but on this night in 1981, it meant that my band mates and I were blowing off a little steam (and maybe some Mexican pot) after our most recent dealings with Roth and Co. had gotten out of control.

We found ourselves on an eight day break and the next tour stop was in Milwaukee, giving us huge amounts of time to get there from Inglewood. A map of the country shows an obvious route, a northeast heading would have made the most sense for us. In retrospect,

I'm sure that Dildo probably tried to dissuade us from taking a more southerly route, but being boys born and raised in New England, we relished a chance to hit any part of the exotic climes of north Texas.

Let's talk now about riding in a tour bus (or a smoke billowing camper) with four or five other males for months on end. Even if you've known these guys from birth, which was pretty much true in our case, you learn things about them that you don't want to know. And early on you realize that the idea of bringing lots of porn movies into an all male environment is a mistake. Uncomfortable silences follow the viewings of such classics as *Chained Virgin Nurse*, and *Backdoor to Paradise* and soon the sport turns more towards chess, Scrabble and endless rehashings of the previous gig.

But in spite of that, after months on tour a fellowship grows that is hard to describe. I've got your back, you've got mine. My dad was a decorated World War II hero and I know you can't trivialize the war experience by comparing it with the traveling nitwit express of rock tours, but something builds up over time that makes you bond.

After a few weeks, you feel like a roving gang of pirates...give us your women and we won't hurt you. It's a stupid respect that rock bands get, even from bikers who should know better, but we in the rock world (if we told you the truth) would say that even the meekest of us dig this vibe. Because, I have to be honest, my band is about as physically intimidating as that French poodle your aunt had put down for snapping at people. But this ladies and gentlemen is ROCK N' ROLL, and though it's just another art form, for some reason it's always scared the straighter types.

We've played on the same bill with probably a few hundred bands, but the band I remember as scaring the most people was The Ramones. Please understand what I mean. In any audience there is a general breakdown of fandom; some true believers and some casual concert goers. Unlike me, Joey Ramone never dressed like a nun, brought women on stage, or took his clothes off during a performance, but damn, that skinny bastard seemed to scare the casuals. Anyone who knew Joey even a little, knew what a sweetheart he was, but onstage, his stance and style seemed to scare some of the folks raised on Beatles and Stones.

Did a Pablo Picasso painting scare the people who were raised on Monet? Maybe yes, if they were looking for a comfort zone. But in every art form, artists come along who don't follow the rules, to the point where they sometimes trash all that went before. Sometimes during vibrant times, an art form gets a vibe about it that makes it seem dangerous; jazz had this, Pablo had it, and rock music sometimes has it. I do know this about rock n' roll; if you walk into an all night greasy spoon full of truckers at three in the morning after ten hours on the road, and you've got your band and roadies at your side, you feel respect and equal footing. Yeah they could kick your ass, but maybe in their minds, at the cost of contracting rare forms of sexually transmitted diseases.

We are all just people on the highway of life. But it's more than that; it's that weird rock band thing. It's like if you're a rocker, you could "go mental" at any point. And three days into our easterly swing, we are definitely going mental.

We had just entered the panhandle area of Texas in the early afternoon hours of June 24, 1981 when we started to take notice of The Big Texan signs that seemed to span the highway every mile or two. *The Big Texan, Home of the Free Seventy-two Ounce Steak- 48 Miles, The Big Texan, Best Bar in Texas-45 Miles.* I'm sure you get the idea.

You must understand that this part of Texas is so friggin empty, flat and boring that if they told you there was a Paper Clip Museum in ten miles you'd probably want to stop and see it. And so we did.

There's a giant cowboy boot out in front of the place,

and floppy hatted people on stilts, dressed to look like giant cowboys. The real feature of the joint was the seventy-two ounce steak that is free if you can eat it all. If you can't eat it all, you pay your sixty bucks and reflect on your own gluttony. Only a few hundred people have completely "eaten the big one" in all the years The Big Texan has been open, but still people come to give it a try.

Though the nine of us are hungry, none of us is tempted by the enormous and potentially expensive piece of cow flesh. We are however fascinated by some of the other items on the menu which include fried rattlesnake, prairie oysters and chicken fried steak. For Northeast boys, these foods are exotic fare. The chance to eat rattlesnake, or exotic animal parts was a rare treat, like giving a cheeseburger to an Eskimo.

We are all set to order when a waitress passes our table carrying a huge glass apparently filled with alcohol. We scour the menu to find out that it's called The Big Tex and it's essentially a twenty-four ounce margarita meant to be shared by at least a few people. Undaunted by the math problem this might present, seven of us order our own Big Tex margarita. Over the course of the next hour we drink, we eat, and we drink again. It can be quite alarming to watch people you've entrusted your musical career to crawling around under tables and behaving like pinheads, but at the same time if you toss away all hopes of survival it can be stupidly uplifting.

This might be a good time to get introductions out of the way so let's go around the table once and meet everyone. First of all there's me, Mike; skinny, curly haired, drunk, and at the moment totally engrossed in seeing how many drink straws I can fit into Walter's hair. Walter is our guitar tech and house sound man. He spent a good part of the previous night taking most of Fritz's money in a poker game and he's currently either sleeping or passed out, head down on the table. I put so many drink straws in his hair that he looked like a man with a religious halo.

Next to him is the aforementioned Fritz, who as usual is remaining somewhat aloof from the current debacle, although he has made several straw gathering trips for Mike.

To his right is our lead guitar player Rich. Aside from being, at times, a brilliant guitar player, he is more known to the band for being able to encapsulate an evening or an adventure with very few words. Once after a bad performance of ours, he wrote this simple graffiti on a dressing room wall; "we came, we played, we sucked." He is currently engaged in a drunken gear conversation of many words about guitar amps with our other guitar player, Stacey.

Stacey and I have known each other since we were five years old. We grew up practically next door and you'd think because of our lifelong friendship, we'd have little about which we disagree. But the opposite is true: we argue about everything-who went out with which girl first, what actor starred in whatever movie, who played bass in Bill What-the-fuck's band, who won the last game of Scrabble and by how much. Our battles rarely get heated, but they do seem to irritate nearly everyone within earshot.

Next to Stacey is an empty chair. That's because Doug, our bass player, is under the table having gone down there to tie Walter's shoelaces together. Next to Doug is another empty chair because Chris, who is our drummer, and also Stacey's brother, went under the table to watch and now the two of them are quite comfortably sitting there talking about baseball, having entirely forgotten the reason for their move. More on them later.

The final two chairs are occupied by Matt, our drum roadie, who is currently finishing his rattlesnake, and Dildo who is wondering how he can get us all back into the campers with a minimum of incidents or arrests. His job is to walk the fine line between authority figure and trusted confidant, but because he has recently sided on more than one occasion with Van Halen's stage manager, an evil power loving rat prick of a person, he is doing neither well and his hold on us is crumbling.

The talk then turned to the possibility of getting another Big Tex. "Just one for the table that we can share," I said aloud, as if this is my own discovery and not the intended use of the huge drink. Matt however saved the day when he loudly remembered seeing a fireworks store on the way into the restaurant located right next door. The thought of buying fireworks galvanizes us to action and soon, like happy, drunken lemmings we exited the restaurant and make our way to the place of big, loud noises. This is the genius of Texas: put a fireworks store next to a drinking establishment.

Where I now live in New Hampshire you must claim to have a rodent problem to acquire fireworks of any power or noise. But back then in Texas you just had to walk up and burble a drunken syllable or two and you could purchase some impressive fire power. We're not talking weapons of mass destruction, but we are talking some big, loud, crazy shit.

So after buying enough ordnance to attack and take over a small South American town, we wandered back to our campers, Walter bringing up the rear, barefoot and with his tied together shoes slung over his shoulder. In short order we are back on the highway. Camper one held Matt, Walter, Chris, and Dildo, who is driving. In camper two there was Rich, Doug, Stacey and me with Fritz behind the wheel. It was now early evening in northern Texas and before long, we in camper two noticed that a firecracker has been thrown out of camper one, most likely by Chris. It landed near our front tires and exploded. This would be the only issuance from camper one during the upcoming battle, but our driver Fritz sets the tone when he says "the bastards are bombing us."

This was an affront that only morons could have perceived but instantly beers are put down (yes, there was more drinking) and the air vent in the roof of our camper was opened. We had no hope of hitting camper one, which was now about fifty yards ahead of us, so ours would be more a show of force. Soon flares, bottle rockets and whirling dervishes filled the night Texas sky above our speeding camper. Doug, always one to push an envelope, decided that we weren't showing off enough shock and awe and opened the side door. Sky rockets, M80's, and roman candles now blazed from our mid-ship, blasting the roadside like a Spanish galleon run amok.

With both the roof and side door spewing pyrotechnics, we must have been a most spectacular sight, and I'm guessing that it was around this time that Dildo, driving camper one, looked in his rear view mirror. The poor man, probably lost in thought, looked up in ashen horror to see the Hindenburg exploding behind him. He immediately pulled over to the side of the road next to an abandoned gas station followed closely by a sheep faced Fritz in camper two.

As we all spilled out of our camper laughing, coughing, our clothes dotted with tiny burn marks, and some small parts of our camper still smoldering, I had the realization that goddammit, this was what rock n' roll was all about. It wasn't about all the crazy Van Halen nonsense, or the pressure from our

record company to "straighten out and write hits."
And it sure as hell wasn't about living up to some
pre-conceived plan we never had about making it
big. It was about surviving to do what you want to
do, in spite of all the bullshit, in the way you want
to do it. Sure, we wanted to get to where we could
do music all the time, but over the years we've all
had to supplement our incomes in any number of real
world jobs.

As I stumbled around the corner to take a
leak, I felt like any pirate captain must have felt
when thinking about the next port of call. Look out
Milwaukee, here we come! I'd like to say that I then
got lost in a Texas moon but the truth is, at that time,
I might have spaced out looking at a spider's web. In
any event when I came back around the corner, both
campers were heading off into the star-filled night
and I was left there alone.

There is nothing so deflating as feeling like
a pirate captain one moment, and in the next like
Captain Bligh in a rowboat watching the Bounty sail
off without you. Remember, this was a time before
cell phones and I had no way to reach my traveling
companions. I must admit that I had some paranoid
thoughts at that moment about Dildo. Maybe it was his
idea to get us drunk and lose us one at a time across
America…and when he finally arrived in Milwaukee
with an empty camper and someone asked where
the band was he would stare at them blankly and say
"band…what band?"

Perhaps this was the kind of thing he'd been doing for years, dispersing opening acts individually around America where their dazed and confused looks would only get them mistaken for homeless people. Maybe all the while we were drunkenly attacking the Texas sky with fireworks, he was quietly planning this moment. Who knows how many bands had gone trustingly out into the world with this maniac never to be heard from again. It was like one of those eighties slasher flicks where the killer dispatches his hapless victims one by one...except for the lack of actual slashing, dead victims, or even a hockey mask.

In my delirium, I even managed to convince myself that stopping at The Big Texan was his idea. It was while I was laying there on top of a dumpster, planning some hideous revenge, that I must have fallen asleep because the next thing I remembered was waking up and there he was, a look of incredible relief on his face. He'd apparently stopped somewhere down the road to get gas and realized he was one Fool short of a band. My band mates in camper two thought I had moved to camper one and never gave it a second thought. I later learned that Dildo had even prevented Doug from tossing one of the remaining M80s (which were only slightly less powerful than a hand grenade) into the dumpster to wake me up.

I never ended up liking Dildo, but I stopped disliking him at that moment, and almost respected him. It's not always about what you think it is. It could be that most of us go through much of life clueless, paranoid, and behind. But that's not me. I've always been right, about everything, all the time. Except maybe record companies...and management...and what songs to write and record...and whether to use a latex or oil based primer on exterior unpainted wood. But life is to learn.

So, now that we've broken the ice, we are The Fools and this is our story...kind of, sort of...I mean, I'm going on memory here, and memory can be admittedly self-serving...but here it is anyhow, in vivid black and white.

CHAPTER TWO

Pedrick's Hole

"If you're gonna screw up, do it while you're young.
Older you get, the harder it is to bounce back"
American author Winston Groom

'Too many people grow up, that's the trouble with the world.'
Walt Disney

Like The Beatles had Liverpool, like Elvis had Memphis and like SpongeBob Squarepants had Bikini Bottom…so The Fools have Ipswich.

Nestled along the coast in the mountainous coal mining region of northeast Massachusetts, Ipswich is not only the birthplace of the American patriot Patrick Henry, but as every schoolchild knows, the generally acknowledged birthplace of the American Revolution.

It was here that the Miner's Revolt of 1746 first challenged Britain's control of the colonies. Tired of twenty hour days and bad working conditions, the miners one day refused to venture down into the mines. What they demanded was an eighteen hour day, a time to eat food and the right to use real picks and shovels instead of pointed sticks made from tree branches and broom handles. The resulting dispute ended favorably for locals and sowed the seeds of dissension that would flourish twenty plus years later.

Coal mining remained the major industry for the next two hundred years, in spite of a handy nearby ocean teeming with fish. The general consensus of the townsfolk seemed to be that fishing was a dangerous and iffy business. I mean why would anyone risk Neptune's fury when they could simply venture hundreds of feet down into the earth and scrape up buckets of black rock from cramped places. "Fish come and go with the tide, but coal doesn't," was the clever saying of the times. This saying was so popular in Ipswich that it could often be found on wooden carvings in many eighteenth century homes.

The fortunes of the town changed dramatically around 1940 when it was discovered that the clam was edible. Prior to this, the clam was considered nothing but a stinky and gooey nuisance, but soon people were baking, broiling and steaming the meaty little mollusk as a food staple. The "peanut fell into my chocolate" moment didn't happen until 1956 when an unnamed fry chef mistakenly dropped a few clams into the fryer giving birth to the fried clam and a major tourist industry. No longer would a few tourists straggle into town each year to view the entrance to Pedrick's Hole, a boring 1,400 foot deep mine shaft. In fact, so many people now flock to Ipswich each year that it has become nationally known as "The Home of the Fried Clam."

It must now be said that there is no better pairing than fried clams and cold draft beer. If you ever decide to visit Ipswich, a good place to enjoy this treat is at Pedrick's Bar; which also has a good view of nearby Pedrick's Hole, thereby combining the breadth and scope of any visiting tourist's itinerary.

A great man once said, "I drink to make other people interesting." I think it was either Ben Franklin or maybe Dean Martin....I don't know I get all the great partiers in history mixed up, but in any case whoever said it would have found Ipswich a most interesting place.

The town joke used to be that bars almost outnumbered churches. But once the happy hour was instituted and the churches neglected to follow suit, it was no longer even a contest. In a town of twelve thousand people, there are close to fifty places to quench your thirst.

Once you remove children from the equation (and you have to because after all this isn't Europe) that's about one bar for every fifteen people. The bars range from spacey, modern places with an ocean view, to dark, guilty spots with four stools and a dusty TV in the corner. Whatever the atmosphere, these places are the glue that brings the townspeople together. After a long day of digging coal, clams or the new local microbrew, they can talk politics, sports, music, beer or who's boinking whom, all while enjoying an adult beverage. It's not a bad life.

As is the case in many working class towns, culture and the finer arts often take a back seat to survival but there have been some proud moments. John Phillip Souza, the world renowned military march king, came to town in 1913 and played three songs on a small orchestra stand hastily built adjacent to a bar next to the train station. Upon the completion of the three marching tunes, he and his band popped into that bar for some elbow bending and later that day departed (to cheers) for the next whistle stop. Someone made the observation that the partying lasted longer than the performance. Maybe his was the first touring rock band.

And let's not forget that the Great American Novelist, John Updike, made his home here in the seventies and eighties and wrote what many consider to be his best work. From a small room above a bar, overlooking another bar on Main Street, he wrote *"Sex with Smart Women," "Sex with Other People's Wives," "Sex with Rabbits,"* and the Pulitzer Prize winning classic, *"Sex, Basketball and Rabbits."*

Around this time period, it was quite entertaining to see him walk through the downtown area and watch the reaction of the townsfolk. The man washing a store front window would try and act as if he were above such work and destined to be a character in some writer's book. The cop writing a parking ticket would stop and strike a reflective pose, or most entertaining to us younger lads, a pretty woman in a low cut top would find a reason to stop and bend down to adjust her shoe. At the time

I remember thinking what a crazy thing it must be to live the celebrity life, but years later I would get a glimpse of it firsthand.

This was the town we Fools were born into, and though we've all known each other since almost birth, we came to music from different directions.

For bass player Doug Forman, it was a ticket out of the coal mines and a way to exploit what, up till then, had seemed a freakish toss of nature's dice. Born with six fingers on his left hand, he spent much of his youth trying to hide the deformity, and working in a dark coal mine was a means to this end. But at some point a high school music teacher had the enterprising thought to put the strange appendage to good use and handed Doug a bass guitar.

The transformation was instantaneous; no longer would he try and hide the offensive digit-he would become a bass player. And though he entered this new career confidently, early band photos often show him with "the hand" in his pocket. Somewhat of a practical joker, later in life he developed a routine he would use on a record exec, a disc jockey or a member of the foreign press.

It went like this: when asked, for instance, about his favorite bands, or foods or baseball players, Doug would always come up with a list of six and begin counting them off on his fingers. "Number one, Babe Ruth, number two, Ted Williams," and so on until he got to number five. At that point he would pause dramatically-and instead of holding up the first finger on his other hand to finish his list, he would say "number six, Lou Gehrig" and flash the fluky finger. More than one victim of the pinky prank was seen stepping back in an uncomfortable attempt to put more distance between themselves and the unholy hand of Doug Forman. This was the man who would be my writing partner during the early years of the band.

I don't think it's a surprise to anyone that showbiz in general and rock n' roll in particular tended to attract the more high strung members of

society. Having said that, it's hard for me to add anything about lead guitar Rich Bartlett that wasn't covered extensively in the hit cable show *Before They Were Stars*, but in case you missed it, I'll re-cap.

I think that there was no glossing over the fact that Rich was a somewhat

Rich in his Ravi Shankar phase

troubled youth, having dropped out of high school in the tenth grade, and the episode on guitar players dealt with this. It seemed unfair that the program only talked to one of his high school friends, and only then on the condition that his voice was disguised and his name and whereabouts were not given.

According to this alleged friend, "Rich was always pissed off about something; he didn't like school, he didn't like sports, and to tell you the truth, I don't think he liked me much either. The only two things he really liked were girls and rock n' roll. Actually the guy was nuts, but you didn't hear that from me," said the nervous man with a slight lisp that even a voice modulator could not hide. (I'm guessing from this evidence that the friend was Chester 'Cheesy' Stilton who I've recently found out lives in Salem, MA.).

Others however could have painted a different story; of a young truth seeker so fed up with society that for a time he lived homeless in the streets. Because they were warm, he often slept in subway stations where he also found some comfort in the deafening noise. In summer months, to keep from being bothered by police, he slept in front of the local Ticketmaster. Who knows how many times he was first in line for a show he had no intention of going to. But it was in one of these ticket lines that, one day, young Rich had a life changing moment.

Deafeningly loud rock music was playing and

there were countless pretty women standing in line. "I must learn to do this," thought Rich, and he did, with a single mindedness that only the slightly unbalanced can muster. The rest is guitar history.

Perhaps the Pedrick brothers, guitar player Stacey and drummer Chris, came to rock music in the most direct and natural way since they were already town celebrities. It was their great, great, etc., grand-dad Wilbur Pedrick who was the first local entrepreneur to capitalize on the rich coal vein running beneath the town. Pedrick's Hole is of course named after him.

Succeeding generations of Pedrick's, while reaping the substantial financial benefits of his actions, have also labored under the unfortunate naming of his project. "Hey, Pedrick, how's your hole?" or worse yet, "Hey, Pedrick, how many guys were in your hole last night?" were the taunts that came with their local celebrity status.

For Chris, these jibes fell upon uncaring ears. He had long since weighed the benefits of great wealth against the cat calls of the have not's, and found the latter wanting. "Fuck you," his lack of response seemed to say, but in fact his head was more than likely filled with numbers. Not just the numbers relating to the family fortune, but all numbers relating to anything that numbers could relate to. Baseball stats, Pythagorean theorems and snowflake duplication probabilities all filled his skull near to the breaking point. He would walk through town lost in calculation, as if all the bars, clams or famous authors in creation could not distract him from his thoughts.

But one day something did. Chris, a rock fan from his earliest memory, was listening to 'Manic Depression' by Jimi Hendrix and after the song was over, the radio voice said that it was done in a 3/4 time signature. It was the first time he'd ever heard someone make a connection between numbers and music. Holy shit thought Chris, or something of the like, and soon he was mentally investigating the possibility that he would play drums in a rock band. All indicators pointed to yes, and they were right.

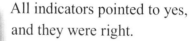

They say the apple doesn't fall far from the tree. So either this tree was really big, wide and unusual, or one these apples might really have been a pear if you catch my drift, because these brothers could not have been more different. While Chris was intense and quiet, Stacey was cheerful yet complicated. His early years are filled with confusing tales of boundless yet misguided endeavors. As a precocious ten year old, when told about the concept of a rock garden, young Stacey spent countless hours tending to a rocky patch in his back yard. Weeding, watering and adjusting the rocks just so to get the proper sunlight.

He worked diligently for a full year until his measurements told him the awful truth: the rocks were the same size as when he started. "What the fuck," was his most likely response. But it was the

artist in him that kept him going, through all the heart breaking fads that were to follow. Ant farms, hula hoops and eight track tapes all struck his fancy, but didn't take hold. Mexican jumping beans, pyramid power and the metric system soon followed in the long order of passing fancies that would tantalize him, but not grab him by the short hairs.

That all changed during the mid-sixties British Invasion of rock music. Stacey had already learned the fundamentals of guitar playing during the "Learn to Play Guitar Like the Ventures" fad earlier in the decade, but now with the apparent staying power of rock n' roll, he'd found a place to be.

Okay I have to stop here...I don't know why I did it, but I just invented total bullshit histories for a bunch of people that I really care about. Yes the Ipswich stuff is mostly true and some of the Pedrick stuff, but why would I lie about the lives of my longtime musical friends? I've thought about this for at least five minutes and, to be honest, I realize that I've never felt the responsibility to tell the public the truth...about anything... at any time... you have been warned... but the next part, where I tell my story, is true... all of it... I promise.

I must say that I'm a little uncomfortable talking about my own personal history; it's often hard to maintain objectivity while being alternately thrilled or pounded and pummeled by memories of certain past incidents. Let's just admit that the autobiographical format is flawed and move on, giving me whatever benefits of the doubt I may be entitled to. I suppose I could have asked one of the other band members to tell my tale, but frankly they're all still a little bit steamed at how I've portrayed them. [Jeezus, Rich, give it up will ya? You were one scary dude in high school-just admit it and move on...]

Maybe the only way to tell my story is in the third person, so here goes: Mike was born, the last of seven children, in the Lower East Side slums of Ipswich. A sensitive, some would say almost saintly child, he seemed ill fitted to the rough and tumble life of a coal mining town. His father, Kareem Abdul Girard, who adopted that name after a brief fling with the Muslim religion, worried about his young son's toughness and soon cultivated techniques to

strengthen him. Whether it was tying a pork chop around his neck and tossing him to the neighborhood dogs, or bungee cording him hundreds of feet down a mine shaft, the elder Girard never seemed to tire of trying to toughen up his young toddler.

By the time Mike reached the age of seven, he had developed not only amazing speed, but excellent bladder control. It was around this time that his mom, Idabelle, in an effort to make ends meet, devised her ill-fated 'Rent a Kid' business. Her thinking went like this: there were probably people out there who wanted a kid, but just for a day or two. Maybe there was a children's movie they wanted to see or, better yet, maybe they were wondering

about having a child of their own and wanted a no-risk tryout. In spite of her innocent intentions, the authorities soon put a stop to the venture. But not before Mike was rented to a wealthy couple from the upscale northern lakes region of Ipswich. It was here that he learned of the pleasures that a well heeled existence can bring. Whether it was lawn bowling, water skiing or the simple joy of eating a pork chop without fear of attack, the young lad felt he was finally in his element. Years later he would remember this period of time as an awakening; an epiphany of sorts...though, at the time, he could neither pronounce the word nor knew what in the hell it meant.

By the time Mike entered high school, his speed had attracted the attention of the football coach, and though he would go on to star as a running back, his real first love was music. And that's all of the third person story telling I can handle, so let's join me at my first job.

I was sixteen and working at a local coffee house called The Kings Rook washing dishes and bussing tables. This meant bringing strong, bad tasting coffee and little plates of stale cheese and crackers to stoned out folkies. Usually, the entertainment ran along straight folk music lines; Joni Mitchell, Tom Rush, and Chris Smither all played there, but sometimes there was a blues band.

I was paid a meager wage, and folkies aren't renowned for tipping well, but while working there I ate my fill of stale cheese and crackers and saw some world class performers. None better than the night the J. Geils Blues Band showed up. This was early Geils, before they recorded their first album, before they knocked off the rough edges and even before keyboardist Seth Justman joined the band.

The coffee house was owned by a well-to-do old

goat who treated us like slaves and seemed to think we were privileged to be allowed entry into his world. One of my duties was to bring the artist(s) whatever amount of stale cheese and crackers they wanted. The owner would say, "Bring them up some cheese," as if I was about to bestow upon them an amazing culinary treat.

Many folk performers back then had an angst and seriousness about them that made you uncomfortable while you were 'delivering the cheese.' It was like "leave it over there, son, the world is too fucked up to put the cheese anywhere else." I was a young man and smoking pot at the time and I found these people hysterically funny. But as I brought the pre-show cheese to the Geils Band, they seemed a happy lot, not worried about much except playing excellent music…and play excellent music they did.

Few people are able to own the stage. I'd seen Muddy Waters do it, I'd seen Mick Jagger do it, and since that night I've seen many men and women take over the stage like they built it themselves. But on that night, to my young eyes, there was no one with more presence and style than lead singer Peter Wolf, and his harp player Magic Dick wasn't far behind.

Some of us in life show up fully formed: The J. Geils Band was an example. At the time I was singing in a run of the mill cover band and after seeing Geils, I seriously wondered if I should give it all up…but I didn't. Years later The Fools had the great pleasure of playing with the Geils Band on more than one occasion, not only in the Boston area, but in Detroit, where they were bigger than anyone and anything; hubcaps, NASCAR, and even home town rock hero Bob Seger.

The year was 1970 and some other people weren't giving up either. The great Brad Delp of the iconic band Boston was making heating elements for Mr. Coffee and maybe wondering if this would be his life when he met two guys named Tom Scholz and Barry Goudreau.

Ben Orr left Cleveland, where he was a well known but no longer respected child star in a TV created Monkees type band, and headed for Columbus to make a new start. There he met Ric Ocasek, they relocated to Boston and before too long, The Cars were born.

Where would rock n' roll be without the bands that resulted from these meetings? Obviously somewhere else, but maybe the point is that it's not about the hits they made, but the fact that they didn't quit on a dream.

CHAPTER THREE

Who invited the Monkeys?

"It has yet to be proven that intelligence has any survival value."
Arthur C. Clarke

Have you ever pissed off a crowd of thousands of people to the point where they made rude noises and pelted you with whatever they had at hand? It's obviously not a common hazard in most lines of work. Neither a house painter nor a chef would experience this no matter how bad a job they did. Most of us know of a lawyer or a politician somewhere who might deserve it, but even the worst of them are mostly just sneered at. Oddly enough, it seems that people save this special treatment for performers. Whether they are baseball players, comedians, or rock bands, if they fuck up according to the standards we set for them, we show them no mercy.

On the night of August 23, 1978, the standard the nine thousand people at the Civic Center in Portland, Maine set for us was simple: "We are not here to see your band, we are here to see the Doobie Brothers. Play your stuff quickly, don't bother us, and get off the stage before our drugs wear off."

These were very clear guidelines, and we clearly understood them, but to that point in our young lives it was the biggest show we'd ever played and we wanted to demonstrate what we were all about.

We knew heading in that we were not your average backup band; along with our punched up pop music there was always a certain amount of shtick (which for those not in the know is a Yiddish word meaning comic theme or gimmick) and even the odd costume change by me. This was the aspect of the band that a manager and a major record company would soon try to eliminate, essentially saying to us, SHUT UP AND PLAY MUSIC.

Before this show we even discussed playing it straight, but it seemed to be the coward's way out. We would go on and do what we goddamn do goddamn it because this was who we were and there was no turning back now! As we hit the stage most people were still finding their seats and a hum of excitement filled the arena. Though we were starting to get known in the Boston area, Portland, Maine might as well have been Spain for all these people knew of us. We would eventually play in Madrid and feel more at home than this night in Maine.

And so, full of foolish confidence in the path we had chosen, we blasted into our first song, 'Spent the Rent', a choppy little number about being broke but partying anyhow. The song was followed by a smattering of polite applause. The arena lights were only now dimming and some people still had their backs to us. Next came 'College Girl,' a song about a small town dirtbag trying to score some educated, upscale ass.

A low grumble followed this song, as if the audience felt tricked, and a boo or two could be heard from the cheap seats. It's funny how that works; three or four people booing in an undecided but already grumbling crowd can give you a general feeling of unease, as if that slight bump on the horizon could be a huge wave coming at you.

Different show...same helmet...

Song number three of our set was where we'd planned our first bit of frivolity, and it was here that the tsunami hit and the wheels began to fall off of our little clown car. The song was called 'WWII' and just as the crunchy power chords started it, I jumped behind an amp for my first costume change. I re-emerged wrapped in an American flag, playing a broomstick as if it were a guitar, and wearing a metal army helmet. This would win them over, I just knew it. I leaped into the first verse,

"Jap Zero in a dead dive, I can't get warm enough in the stinking jungle. God damn army chow, another fuckin' stoned bummer Let me tell you 'bout Sheila oh yeeeeea!"

What had simply been general distaste started to turn towards open hostility as the crowd, appalled at our attempts to entertain them, booed, jeered and collectively flipped us off. Undeterred by their bad manners, we ground into the second verse:

"Smells bad livin' in a foxhole, can't find my cig-a-rettes. Hey, Kawalski keep your fuckin' head down You want me then go take a number oh yeeeea!"

People were now jumping up and down, and waving their arms, as the first cup of beer hit the stage and doused my pants. Throwing that beer at us seemed like a good idea to others and soon all manner of objects began landing around us. Beer cups, empty food containers and ball point pens rained down upon us. Loose change, belt buckles, and even a friggin' lawn dart landed at my feet (even now I often wonder what kind of person brings a sharp pointy flying object to a concert).

It wasn't like the crowd disliked us; no they fucking hated us and wanted us to die. How weird is it that we let so many important things pass in life, but we seem to say "Don't fuck with my leisure time." Years later, when I was on tour in Europe, we visited a zoo in Germany and saw a group of monkeys jumping, screaming and throwing their feces at anyone who came close to their cage, I would remember this crowd.

By the time Rich got to the guitar solo, the entire band was ankle deep in debris and moving carefully on stage to avoid drawing any further fire in our direction. I remember looking at the other guys and realizing that they weren't afraid. The irony of the situation was classic: we were playing a song about soldiers in a foxhole, and here we were in our own foxhole getting bombarded.

At that point our choices were simple; either walk off the stage and don't ever play again because we obviously sucked, or find a way through the night and maybe even enjoy the moment. We decided to stay.

Just before the war song ended, someone from high above, or far away, threw one of those pot pipes made from small metal plumbing parts. It clanged off the top of my helmet and for the next couple of songs there were some notes I couldn't hear, but we finished the set.

I wish I still had the dented helmet. I've told many people this story and they listen sympathetically until I tell them that the experience was somehow exhilarating, and then they think I'm nuts. This is how I see it: if the whole night had been a smattering of applause after each song, accompanied by general audience boredom and indifference, I would look back at it as a dismal failure.

After our set the Doobies' guitarist Skunk Baxter came into the dressing room and said "that was fucking great!" He then asked if we wanted to come on stage during their encore. I found this to be a supreme kindness from someone who owed us nothing, but I said something like "thanks but you don't need us up there."

The Doobies then went on and played one major hit after another, for two hours, including most appropriately for that night 'What a Fool Believes.' During their second or third encore, after they had thanked and gotten ovations for not only the mayor, and the arena staff, but the floor mats and chairs, Skunk yelled out "let's hear it for the Fools!" It was the only down moment in two hours of adoration as people almost growled their confusion and displeasure at their hero's mention of the evil jesters who had earlier polluted the stage.

It's an odd thing to be booed, pelted and publically flogged for playing music people haven't been trained by radio to like, but within six months we were getting airplay on Portland radio stations and backing up Rush in the very same arena to probably many of the same people; but this time to an encore. The lesson I learned from the experience was this: it's sometimes good to challenge the format, but always remember to wear a sturdy helmet.

CHAPTER FOUR

Too lazy for work, too dumb
for school, let's start a band

I was painfully shy as a kid, and other than girls, sports, music and girls, there wasn't much else that lit me up. I had a certain amount of athletic ability so playing sports kept me busy, and I loved to sing. Only my closest friends knew I could sing, because like most introverts, though I was unable to raise my hand in a classroom, amongst my friends I was a loud, obnoxious, pain in the ass. And where does a boy end up who's afraid of crowds, but is a wise ass and loves music and women? I can almost hear you scream the answer - A ROCK BAND!

It all began one day when I was fourteen. Stacey mentioned that he wasn't able to find a singer for the band he was starting, and asked if I would like to give it a try. I said yes, and within a week, I sang a Yardbirds' song at an Ipswich teen dance. The rest of the set the band played surf instrumentals.

Within two weeks we entered and almost won a North of Boston battle of the bands. Each of the ten bands played two songs. That worked for us because that's all I'd had time to learn. The bands were not only judged on music, but ridiculous categories like neatness and presentation. We went on dressed in matching slacks, shirts, belts and ties. At that point in my life, I was pencil thin and it was hard to find an adult looking belt that didn't wrap around me twice. We went on and as I looked out at the hundreds of cheering people in the audience, I remember wondering if it was normal to crap yourself in situations like this.

But we played the tunes, I made it through our set and the audience genuinely seemed to like us. The four judges rated us highly in all categories except neatness. In an unintended prequel to the risqué performances I would give in later years, I went on stage forgetting to run my belt through one of its loops, and it dangled obscenely between my legs throughout our two songs.

Since even second place was something we'd never expected, we took the night as a victory and went home to learn some more songs. For the rest of high school, I sang in one cover band or another, standing stock still, looking at no one, making sure my belt was looped, and trying my best to sound like the singer in whatever song we were playing. The bands were passingly decent, and most times when songs ended, people would clap. It seemed like a good exchange. At times I would try and imitate the confidence I'd seen in the performers at the coffee house, but these early attempts at a stage persona were embarrassing at best.

The only time I'd talk to the audience was if someone asked me to read an announcement, and then I would grudgingly take the paper, affect a stern tone, and announce that a car had to be moved, or that some kid's mom was here to get them. And even though I had all the stage charisma of a folding chair, I noticed a strange thing starting to happen; girls were talking to me. Sure, maybe it was just to request a song or to ask for a dedication, but it was talking nonetheless. I was hooked.

At around the same time period I witnessed something at the coffee house that both puzzled and amazed me. Once or twice a year, in order to stay on good terms with the locals, the owner, Carlson Pepperdink, would hold a fundraiser for a Boy Scout troop, a Little League team or an old ladies drama club and get some regionally well known person to host it. Usually it was a retired baseball player, or a politician, but this year it was a rather nerdy looking TV weatherman. Since, at that time, there were only three major television stations in the Boston area, he fit the bill as a minor celebrity.

There weren't any dishes to wash, or tables to bus, so I had the great pleasure of standing next to Gloria while she took tickets at the door. Gloria was twenty-two, eight years older than me, a worldly and untouchable blonde Gwen Stefani who constantly popped her chewing gum and seemed oblivious to the nonstop gawking she received from men of all ages. She treated me like a goofy younger brother and once defended me from the owner when I dropped a plate of the precious cheese on my way to a table of stoned out folkies. "But he's so cute," she said, smiling at Pepperdink, who quickly forgot my transgression in the bask of her hundred watt glow.

The event went on as scheduled, a raffle was held, a folk singer sang a song about leaving a woman to "ramble" and finally Pepperdink, in all his pompous glory introduced the weatherman. As I remember him he was thin, fortyish, balding and wore black horn rimmed glasses. He gave a short talk about weather, and how it changed a lot in New England, and how difficult it was to forecast, even harder he said than the stock market. Some people chuckled.

Then he said something about the changing times of man or some such nonsense and finished up with a cautionary tale about the Hurricane of '37. The audience didn't seem confused by this ominous ending, and he left the stage to friendly applause. Soon enough the night was over, people filed out of the club, and I was left to put the tables and chairs back in place. When that was done, I headed upstairs to see if the weather guy had left any cheese or other refuse in the dressing room. I thought he'd already gone so I didn't bother to knock, and I walked in to find Gloria and the weather dude locked in a kiss.

"Out," Gloria simply said, looking over his shoulder. The next day I was too embarrassed to even look at her, but she would have none of it. In between gum poppings she explained the obvious: that I'd seen something I wasn't supposed to see. She was so matter of fact about it that my coloring returned to normal and I couldn't help but ask her, "but why that guy?"

"Because he's famous," she replied matter of factly.

I had no answer for this, but I did walk away wondering if I should pursue a career in meteorology. It's an odd power we give to people we see on television, or in movies, or on stage. The very best carpenter or plumber in the world right now doesn't get a standing ovation at the completion of any given job, but even a barely recognizable bit actor can cause a stir by showing up at some small town coffee shop.

Two hundred years ago it was the very rich who were thought to be better than all the rest of us. Now it's even the nitwit neighbor on a reality show who's signing autographs. Someone once told me that they'd seen Bruce Springsteen play a three hour show. They said they'd never seen anyone work so hard on stage. I tried to tell them that it's neither hard nor work when you're doing something you love and people are adoring you for it.

When high school finished, my career choices were simple; I could either dig coal in a stinky mine, or dig clams in the equally stinky mud. I chose choice two and a half; I would dig clams in the daytime and play in a band at night. Since the drinking age was eighteen back then, night clubs sprang up like mushrooms all around the suburbs of Boston. The common gig was to play a club from Wednesday night to Sunday night, often with a matinee on Sunday afternoon. More than once after a day of clamming I showed up at a gig sunburned, mosquito bitten and smelling slightly of low tide, but always ready to rock.

It was a great environment to learn how to play. By now I was getting a little more comfortable on stage, but I was still throwing up before almost every show, usually after pulling over to the side of the road. Once I threw up on the boots of a state trooper who'd stop to see what was going on.

More cover bands followed with names like The Cold Water Army, and The Magic Twangers. With each new band also came a wider circle of musician friends, and though none of us were writing songs yet, our song list had gotten quite eccentric. In high school bands we played whatever was most popular on the radio, and because of that we gigged a lot. But as our tastes broadened, it seemed less cool to play the popular stuff. We started wanting to play the things we were listening to; an eclectic mix that ranged from The Velvet Underground to Muddy Waters, and as a result, the better the bands got, the less we played.

The band from that time period ('73-'74) that played the least, but was probably the best was called the Rhythm Assholes (Rhythm A's on any marquee) and included Rich on guitar, me on vocals, Steve Cataldo on guitar, Rob Skeene on bass and Jeff Wilkinson on drums. In a year or so from that point, Steve, Rob, and Jeff would form The Nervous Eaters, a seminal Boston punk band, and I would be off to California, but for now we were all just playing the stuff we most liked, whether it brought us gigs or not.

We were a hairy, intense combination of people. I think we all wanted to do something different, but we didn't know exactly what that was. Steve was the first person I met who could write a song that sounded like a complete thought. Jeff was a drummer with a Keith Moon attack on both life and the drums, a creative force who seemed at ease with almost anyone but himself.

Most bands in clubs at the time were playing covers, but there were some notable exceptions. We had all seen The Modern Lovers with their strange but compelling lead singer Jonathan Richman and were blown away by their performance. Best known for the song 'Roadrunner' the pre-punk band also included future members of two of the biggest bands of the eighties; The Cars and The Talking Heads. The Modern Lovers had an edge and originality that other local music at the time lacked.

Jonathan however quickly tired of the rock band thing and wanted to play a gentler style of music. When the Lovers broke up in '74, Jonathan's second home became the basement at Jeff's house where we practiced. He was also playing small coffee house gigs with an acoustic guitar and selling them out. I was intrigued by his stage demeanor; when he talked to an audience he treated them like a fifth grader talking to a third grade class. It all seemed like pretty innocent stuff as he sang 'Hey There Little Insect' and other songs about pets, young love, and abominable snowmen in the supermarket. It was even rumored that he would occasionally cry on stage but I never saw it.

One night he asked if I wanted to sing backup at one his local gigs. I was still pretty stiff on stage, but some part of me wanted to see firsthand what he was doing, so I agreed. I sang with him at three different shows, watched him make children out of adults, and learned that not only was he for real, but that he believed every night on stage would be magical. Many years later people would know him as the singer/narrator in the trees from the great Farrelly Brothers movie *There's Something About Mary.*

Before long Steve Cataldo was adding a few of his originals to our set list. It quickly became apparent that he should be singing his own music and I started thinking about quitting the band and heading out west, where my lifelong friend, Gordie Noble had moved a couple years earlier. By the spring of '74 the decision was made. I converted a Volkswagen bus into a camper, filled it with plants, food, a box or two of my favorite records, a couple of boxes of books, my cat Missy, my girlfriend Ginny and off we went. Within a month we were in northern California and for the first time in my young adult life I was out of a band with no plans to start a new one.

We settled in one half of a small duplex in Boyes Hot Springs, totally oblivious to the available puns the town's name could offer us. Boyes is a tiny town nestled up against Sonoma. Where have you heard that name before? Yes, wine country, but in 1974 it was an industry mostly lacking in national sales. You could still rent an apartment in the area without selling a child or a kidney. Employment was not the easiest thing to find, but Ginny went to work at a tiny place in Sonoma called Mary's Pizza.

Having developed a great many highly specialized skills clamming back in Ipswich, I put them to work and got a job mowing lawns at a trailer park. Over time I would also toil at a leather factory and water grape plants at a winery. It didn't take long for me to realize that menial tasks don't necessarily have to be mind numbing. While standing over one of an endless line of grape plants that needed to be watered, and having run out of things to occupy my mind, I came up with an idea that actually resulted in a song. There seems to be something about giving the mind a simple task that frees up the creative side.

The song, a little ditty called 'WWII,' would become an early Fools' staple. In the years since, I've learned that some great ideas can arrive unbidden while you're mowing the lawn or even driving a car; pretty much any task that doesn't involve expending a great deal of mental energy.

While in California, Ginny and I also learned the great art of living cheaply. We were happy but poor, and the weather was nice. When weekends came and money allowed, we would head into San Francisco to dig the music scene. Our favorite stop was The Boarding House, a cool old joint with squeaky floors and great sight lines. Lou Reed, The Kinks, The Grateful Dead, Neil Young, and many others played shows there. The best radio station at the time was KSAN which much like WBCN in Boston was an original and early founding father of FM radio.

One morning while trying to decide whether a coiled up "thing" thirty feet away was a watering hose or a rattlesnake, an amazing song blasted out from my pocket transistor. 'White Punks on Dope' by The Tubes was an instant sensation in the Bay Area, and it was still only a tape given by the unsigned band to the radio station.

I saw The Tubes for the first time at The Boarding House that weekend, and the mixture of comedy, spectacle and great music was a revelation. The idea that you could create a stage persona out of whole cloth, and change it from song to song, was something that had never occurred to me. The Tubes also validated the notion I'd had that rock n' roll had become an overblown, self important behemoth that was ripe for mockery and satire. The very stance of rock had changed from early balls to the wall, bad boy performers like Jerry Lee Lewis, to louder and louder metal head bands where the priority was to strike a pose and hold it.

In a thousand years, an archeologist looking at

rock performances from the seventies and eighties could only conclude from the grimaces lead guitar players made that it was an incredibly painful undertaking to play the guitar. (By the way, the coiled up 'thing' thirty feet away was indeed an eight foot rattlesnake.)

By the time October came, my irrigation job at the winery evaporated and Gordie found me work at a leather tanning factory in Napa. Gordie was a leather salesman and had some sway with the place. It's still the hardest job I've ever had. My shift went like this: I would show up at seven a.m. and begin loading about a hundred leather hides, weighing from ten to twenty pounds into a huge drum, all the while wearing a rubber suit and boots. Once the hides were loaded in, the door on the drum closed, it filled with tanning chemicals, and it began to spin. By now it was about 9 o'clock and I would spend the next three hours unloading palettes of uncured hides off of trucks.

Most of the work force was Mexican migrant workers and few of them spoke English. The job tended to dictate that people of a certain size and ruggedness would work the drums best. Most of my co-workers looked like heavyweight prize fighters, and even though I was 5'11" and 150 pounds, my nickname was *Miguelito* (little Mike). At around noon, it was time to empty the now soggy hides from the drums.

This was the hard part because each hide now weighed between twenty and forty pounds. You opened the door, fished them out one at a time, and carried them ten feet across a slippery cement floor to stack them on a palette. We were paid for an eight hour day no matter how long our day lasted.

Some of the big guys could empty their drums in a couple hours, meaning they'd only worked seven hours, and bets were made among the best of them on who would finish first. One at a time they would finish and head to the back parking lot; their day's work completed. They'd drink long neck bottled beer and cook up some chicken on a grill.

There was never a bet on who would finish last, but there were probably bets on whether I would finish at all. I would emerge some days at five or six in the evening, knees and elbows scraped and bruised, to the drunken cheers of my co-workers, who seemed to consider me some form of mascot. They'd laugh, hand me a beer and a piece of chicken, and reenact in pantomime one of my more spectacular falls, all to the delight of everyone including me.

I didn't learn many Spanish phrases, but over the course of that winter I learned how to swear. "*Hijo de puta,*" I would yell when a hide slipped out of my gloved hands. "*Gilla pollas,*" I would mutter under my breath when the boss walked by. The first word means motherfucker, the second word means asshole. After a few weeks, with practice and occasional help from one of my new friends, my work day went from eleven hours to around nine. There were Friday nights where I would get home at six, eat something, lay down for a nap and wake up at six the next morning.

After about a month of this hellacious work, I met a guy, originally from Maine, who worked at the other end of the plant. His name was Moe, and he was a big, soft spoken thirty year old guy who treated everyone as an equal. His job was to take the cured hides and trim them individually with a very sharp knife, and separate the good hides from the bad. It turned out that he needed a helper. This was a godsend. Moe and I, being music fans and Red Sox fans, hit it off quickly and soon I was working normal human being type hours.

I didn't know it then, but I was signing on with the leather company legend. Moe liked to bet on things, and soon enough we were betting on whether I could name the artists of four consecutive songs on the oldies station. If I could, he'd pay for our coffee break. If I couldn't, I'd pay. I wasn't the only one he wagered with; other workers came by and there were bets on football games, bets on how many days it would rain in the upcoming month, and bets on the exact minute the lunch wagon would drive up to the back door and stop.

Moe seemed to win a little more than half of his bets, but win or lose, he remained philosophical and even tempered. "I thought I had you on that one," he'd smile and say if he lost. He was, however, very adept at a more high stakes game I came to think of as the lunchtime frolics.

About three weeks after I started working with him, the foreman Manny came over and told Moe, "I got one for you if you want it." Moe smiled and said, "sure, how about Friday after lunch."

"What was that about?" I asked after Manny left.

"He's got a guy for me to fight," Moe said.

"Why would you want to fight somebody?"

"Money," he replied. "We clear out some tables in the cafeteria, everybody bets on who they think will win, and I can make some money."

"But how do you make money on it?"

"Because I bet on me," said Moe slowly, as if explaining something to an idiot.

"But you haven't seen this guy, what if he's good and he beats you?" I stammered, thinking of some of the huge guys I'd worked with at the other end of the factory.

"Then I lose," Moe replied matter of factly.

The day of the fight arrived and you could feel the anticipation and the energy level of the factory ratcheting up as lunchtime approached. Moe didn't seem any different than any other day, and was finishing his sandwich when people started clearing away the tables. Most of the seventy or so workers were in attendance, having made their bets that morning with Manny, as well as most of the upstairs office workers, including the plant manager. These were people we almost never saw, and the fact that the fight appeared to be sanctioned by the company amazed me. Maybe this was a way to boost company morale and blow off a little steam.

Moe stood up, carried his chair to a corner, handed me a towel, and sat down. From the other side of the room his opponent Carlos entered, followed by Manny. The kid was about twenty and at 6'3" and two hundred forty pounds he had Moe by at least twenty pounds and a couple of inches. I'd gone to look at him that morning, before I bet my five bucks. At the time that was a lot of money to me and I didn't think Moe had a chance, but I had to bet on him. Manny took my money and wrote my name on a piece of paper. From what I could gather, Moe was a slight underdog.

Manny now walked to the center of the cleared space and asked if anyone else wanted to bet on the fight. A few people made last minute bets, and finally it was time. He announced that there would be three three minute rounds. If there was no obvious winner at that point, a fourth round would last until one of the fighters couldn't continue.

Manny then gave each fighter a pair of boxing gloves. I nervously helped Moe put his on, tied them up, and he walked out to stand next to Manny to the cheers of everyone assembled. Next, out came Carlos, like Moe, wearing a sleeveless t-shirt, smiling and looking confident to an equal amount of cheers. Manny had them touch gloves and it began.

It was obvious immediately that Carlos had some experience at this sort of thing and he danced sideways flicking out a jab that caught Moe on the cheek. People cheered. Moe moved slowly, hands up and head dodging most of what came his way. Carlos darted in, landed a couple of body shots and a right hook to the temple, now to thunderous cheers and applause. Still Moe had not thrown a punch. It looked like he was about to get embarrassed.

Carlos was feeling it, and he came in close and caught Moe with a left hook. It was the last punch he threw. Moe, a split second after taking the punch, threw his only punch of the fight, an overhand right that caught Carlos flush in the face. Carlos went down like a cut flower. The place erupted; Moe put his arms straight up, nodded his head slightly to acknowledge the cheers and bent down to help the dazed Carlos to his feet. It was one of the most casual acts of confidence I'd ever seen. I asked him later, as he counted out a large pile of cash, his cheek red and swollen, where he'd learned to fight.

"New England Golden Gloves," he said and then we were back to work, cutting hides as if nothing extraordinary had just happened.

There would be a couple more Friday fights

before I left, but not involving Moe. He'd apparently never lost a factory fight, and it was only the occasional new guy, like Carlos, who would take him on. I remembered him asking me one day why I was working there. I couldn't think of a good answer.

"Okay," he said, "name the next four bands and I'll buy coffee on Monday." A few years later, I would have the great pleasure of inviting him and his girlfriend to see us back up Van Halen at the Oakland Coliseum.

I also made friends with the guy who lived in the other half of our duplex. Pat Greene played guitar, drove an old De Soto, was a football fan, and liked a lot of the same music that I did. He too was working hellish hours, so on weekends we drank beer, played music, wrote a couple of songs, and saw whoever we could afford to see. He was with me when I saw The Tubes, and later when Ginny and I saw a Beau Brummels reunion.

One surprise for me was seeing Van Morrison in a small club and realizing that he too had some form of stage fright. Through one marvelous song after another, he stood either sideways, or looked down at the floor, never once saying a word to the audience in between songs. Some may have seen this as arrogance, but I saw it for what it was; a man dealing with his fears the best way he knew how, in order to play his stuff.

Even though Gordie, Pat and I would get

together whenever possible to jam, I was starting to long for the great joy of playing music in a band. By the time spring came, Ginny and I were planning our return to Ipswich. We loved northern California, but the work was hard and if I was going to start a band, it made sense to go back to where I could draw on familiar resources.

The leather factory job would turn out to be the last real employment I would have for the next fifteen years. When I told Moe we were heading back he said, "It's about time. You need any money for the trip?" I told him we were all set and he said, "Good luck with the music. Today I'll pay for coffee break."

CHAPTER FIVE

"You're not Fools, you're assholes!"

On our trip back across the country my head was filled with possibilities. First of all, I had to steal Rich from whatever band he was playing in. I strongly believed that everything after that would fall right into place. And despite the odds, it did. Rich had been playing in a group with the Pedrick brothers, and we recruited Doug Forman because he'd been in the Magic Twangers with Rich, Chris and me.

We immediately started rehearsing cover tunes, and knowing we actually wanted to get paying jobs, this time it was alright if some of them were hits. Back in California, I'd learned what it was like to work really hard and if playing some popular covers would keep us gigging, I had no problem with it. The band would tentatively be called Five Desperate Men.

As luck would have it, we'd only been practicing for a couple of weeks when we got a call from a club north of Boston saying that a band had cancelled and would we like to fill in. "Yes," we said.

And so it was that with only fifteen songs in our repertoire we showed up and found that we would have to play four forty minute sets. By the end of the first set, we'd played all fifteen songs and muddled through some others that we all sort of knew from past bands. By early on in the second set we'd played everything that we knew and the club had emptied out except for the owner.

I'm not sure whether we made a conscious decision to try and bluff our way through the rest of the night, but that's what happened. After all, the club owner didn't know we'd run out of songs, he just knew that we sucked so bad that his club had cleared out. We hoped that maybe if we could make it through the next three sets, he'd still pay us.

So that's what we did. First we repeated most of the first set, trying to change the tempos of songs to make them sound different. 'Brown Eyed Girl' done like a slow blues tune was interesting. Other songs we stretched out by repeating verses and choruses (you'd be surprised how long it takes to actually count the tears in '96 Tears'). Then it was on to TV theme songs like 'Rawhide' and 'The Addams Family.' When those ran out we started doing show tunes like 'Oklahoma' and '76 Trombones.'

Most of the songs probably only sounded vaguely familiar at best; because after singing the title, I rarely knew the rest of the words. The poor band had only brief stretches where they all played the same chord at the same time. It must have sounded like monkeys had broken into a music store, led by an escapee from an asylum. All the while the club owner sat halfway back in his big empty club and watched us with the kind of fascination you'd have if you saw a fat man slowly pull a turtle out of his ass. It was like a gruesome wreck on the side of the road; he desperately wanted to look away but couldn't.

By now we were just flat out having fun. It was on this night that we first played 'Mac the Knife' (which through the years became a regular on the set list) and realized that going "woods bombing," as we came to call it, was a wonderful thing. I think now that if we'd shown up at that gig with fifty cover tunes all worked out, The Fools might never have gotten started. After three sets, the owner called it quits on the night, but-wonder of wonders-he paid us most of what he owed! Within days after this show, we changed our name from Five Desperate Men to Five Desperate Fools, and finally to The Fools.

Our goals after that show were pretty simple: learn enough songs to play a gig somewhere. At the time, there was a small rock club in Ipswich called

The Sunnyside, and being local boys, we thought we'd have no trouble getting in. The songs we'd chosen included some Geils, some Stones, some Kinks, and an eclectic mix of country and blues. It was good danceable stuff that we could live with and I was finally feeling very comfortable on stage.

Our first weekend at The Sunnyside went well and we got hired for some return gigs. I remember looking at the club's upcoming shows and wondering who Cap'n Swing was. Within a year they would change their name to The Cars.

After The Sunnyside, more gigs followed in other local towns like Amesbury, Beverly and Salisbury Beach. Soon we were playing five nights a week on a fairly regular basis. The money wasn't great, but since we'd all moved into some low rent housing in the slums of Ipswich's lower east side, we were able to scrape by. And the price of a gallon of gas in 1976 was just thirty cents…honest to God.

We began printing our own newsletters, which contained dramatic headlines ("Psychic's Head Explodes!!"), upcoming dates and whatever rumors and innuendo we felt like spewing out. The thinking was that if we made them funny and interesting, people would save them when we passed them out at clubs. We all contributed to the funny stuff, but Doug was the main worker bee on getting the newsletter pasted together and printed. It became something that people looked forward to, and it set us apart from other local bands.

Another thing that set us apart from the scene was our general approach to any given night; we expected to come up with a little craziness. Our second stint at The Sunnyside was well attended, and the owner thought it a perfect time to institute a wet t-shirt contest. He told me I would be hosting it on the following night. He was kind of a sleazy older guy, and I didn't like being told instead of asked.

So the next night, during the first set, we made a big announcement about the contest and brought out three t-shirts on hangers. Then we soaked them down, and tried to get people to applaud for the one they liked best. There were more than a handful of disappointed patrons, especially those hard bitten miners in the audience, but for the most part, people were amused.

The owner was not however pleased, and after the set he introduced me to two large breasted, attractive women who, he said, wanted to enter the real contest. I guessed that they were paid strippers brought in by him to get the ball rolling, so we brought up those two, along with a real contestant.

Then Doug introduced me as his blind assistant, and wearing dark glasses and carrying a spray water bottle, I stumbled around the stage spraying everything in my path; Stacey, Rich, one of the women…it was pretty fuckin' funny.

The joke ended when one of the hired pros took the bottle from me and sprayed her own shirt, and then sprayed the other two as well. A winner was chosen, the women left the stage and we played a song. At the end of the song I made an announcement that startled everyone in the band, including me.

"YOU KNOW WE'RE ALL ABOUT EQUAL RIGHTS IN THIS BAND, SO TOMORROW NIGHT, IN ORDER TO EVEN THE SCORE, WE'RE GOING TO HAVE A DRY JOCK STRAP CONTEST!!"

 People laughed and clapped. The guys in the band weren't laughing. Stacey looked at me and said simply, "No." Chris looked up from the drums, a puzzled expression on his face, as if he was replaying what he'd just heard. Rich had decided to ignore the moment; maybe people would forget. Doug however wore a smirk, he knew we'd do it. And we did. The next night the place was jammed, as if people knew that we were going to make good on my promise.

That was the thing about us; you never knew when a night would become unforgettable. Before the start of the second set we had a glib friend announce that the regional finals of the Dry Jockstrap Contest were about to start. We'd written out the things he was supposed to say, and one by one we came on stage to be introduced, all wearing nothing but a jockstrap.

One of us was a plumber from Maine, another was a school teacher from Hamilton, and so on. The place went crazy. It seemed that if we were going to have people cheer for a winner, there should be a clear cut favorite. To that end, prior to taking the stage, Chris put a cucumber down his jockstrap, and became the crowd favorite. He was awarded an all expense paid vacation to Rowley, a tiny town bordering Ipswich. When the contest ended, we put our clothes on and played a song.

More gigs followed and original songs started sprinkling into the show. Doug and I would spend hours working up ideas to bring to the band, but more often than not, the good songs came quickly. One of The Fools' most popular songs 'It's a Night for Beautiful Girls' was something I wrote with the idea that it be a dark, ironic song about a Jekyll and Hyde type of maniac. I didn't think it was working.

Doug helped me put chords to it and we played it

were also some undeniable low points. We once took our act inland to a place called The Red Barn in Westborough. It was the kind of straight down the middle cover club that we had trouble with.

The night we played, it was packed with people expecting to hear the radio songs they loved. Before we started, the club sound system blasted the hits of the day and people filled the dance floor. As soon as we began to play, the dance floor cleared and people sat down and watched us. When the song finished it was deathly quiet; even the crickets had stopped chirping. I tried breaking the ice with a flip comment or two, but they fell on deaf ears. After every song there was a creepy silence, even after the funny stuff. When our set ended, the dance floor once again filled with people, and that's how the night went. Oddly enough there were no boos or catcalls from the crowd, just patent indifference.

During the breaks we took refuge in the dressing room, and tried to figure an angle. Some pot was smoked to take off the edge and we pondered our predicament, but on this night there would be no breakthrough. At the end of the night the manager came in to pay us and flipped out when he smelled the acrid scent of the happy sticks we'd burned in his dressing room. He went on a stunning, screaming, tirade that had us back pedaling out the door. He yelled about his years in the business and how he'd never met such careless, no talent morons as us. And then he finished with this memorable line:

"YOU'RE NOT FOOLS, YOU'RE ASSHOLES! I'LL MAKE A CAREER OUT OF RUINING YOU GUYS!"

However much we may have deserved a stern chastisement, there was no doubt that our unsuccessful night played a big part in his over the top rant. His comment became part of our band folklore. Down through the years, whenever we had a bad night, or something went wrong, we would imagine him, now homeless and nearly destitute from his endless pursuit to ruin our careers; plotting his next move in the dark regions of whatever club we were playing at.

Then there were the places where it took us forever to draw a crowd. The Rusty Nail, a small club in Salisbury, was just far enough away from our home base in Ipswich that we had to build a new crowd there. The manager, a tough as nails guy named Gino, was originally an Ipswich native who took a liking to us and kept us week after week with almost nothing to show for it. At one point we thought of changing the name of the band to Free Lobster, just so we could get a few people through the door.

It got so bad that when one of us absconded with a life-size, cardboard stewardess from Logan Airport in Boston, the first thought was to bring her to the 'Nail, bend her at the waist, name her Heidi, and place her at a table in the dimly lit club. Before long she was joined by cardboard country star Mac Davis, him being stolen by a fan from a record store display.

Some nights we sat them together; Heidi in sunglasses with a drink near her frozen hand, and Mac with an unlit cigarette stuck in the hole we had made in his mouth. On other nights we placed them at separate tables, both obviously heartbroken at the split, but still smiling. And because we were bored, we often placed them in impossible sexual positions, to the point where they'd been bent so much they needed duct tape and splints to sit up straight.

Most of the few people who came to see us knew that Mac and Heidi were inanimate, but once in a while there would be an incident. One night a very drunken biker asked me, "Why the fuck is that guy staring at me?" And I'm sure more than one man did a double take and wondered who the blond babe in the corner was.

Through it all, Gino laughed at our funny stuff, yelled at us if we were too late or too loud, and paid us at the end of every week. He was about ten years older than us, a bald, large block of a man who had a reputation as a street fighter before he left Ipswich. It was said that he once held an off duty cop by his heels from the town bridge in payment for some perceived injustice. No charges were filed and the story became local urban lore amongst the coal miners.

When we finally started to draw people at his

The only known surviving picture of Gino

place, we witnessed his finesse at crowd control. I never saw him throw a punch; he would just get in the face of whoever was a problem and tell them loudly to leave. I remember one large fellow challenging him and saying, "I'm not leaving, and if you touch me I'll sue."

"You'll sue from traction!" Gino yelled as he put his hands in the guy's armpits, lifted him straight up, and walked him backwards out the door. The large fellow never returned.

Within a couple of years, we were too popular for Gino to afford us, but as a way of repaying his kindness to us, we played there one night, let him charge whatever cover he wanted at the door, and charged him $150.00, the price he used to pay us. Later, when we needed a road manager for our first American tour (with The Knack), it was Gino we talked into coming with us. Sometimes the friends you make for life come from unlikely circumstances.

The next year, 1977, saw us playing as far north as Montreal, and south and west into New York. Stacey, the only one of us who had a good business head, was booking the band. We were now doing well enough to hire a soundman and someone to do our lights. Up until then, the ever resourceful Rich had mixed the band from the stage.

We also began to have our own stage vocal monitors, a small speaker pointed towards you that allowed you to hear your voice no matter how loud it got out front. It took a while for me to get used to hearing myself on stage, but I think that not having monitors for years prior to that, made my voice stronger as I'd have to sing louder to hear myself.

Our song list was also growing, both with originals and obscure covers and we were getting better. One night in Bangor, Maine, in order to get a sluggish club crowd onto the floor, I told them that we were going to have a dance contest. This brought out a few couples who gyrated wildly to the song we played. The audience voted on the top three couples and it was time to award prizes.

Since I didn't have any, I grabbed things close at hand. The third place couple won a shoe that I'd found in the parking lot earlier that day. They played along and acted thrilled. The second place couple received a rolled up piece of paper that I said was the deed to the motel across the street. They were also happy. Finally, for the first place couple, I pointed to the beautiful grand piano in the corner of the club, and told them that they'd won it. They seemed delighted. The contest worked and after that the place loosened up and partied for the rest of the night.

After the show, we were in the dressing room when the club's manager burst in and said, "You'd better come deal with this!" Two men, one of whom was part of the winning couple, were pushing the grand piano towards the door, where a flat bed truck awaited.

"What are you doing?" I asked after running over.

"I called my brother 'cause he's got a truck big enough to move the piano," he said happily.

This was bad. "Hey, that was all just a joke! I mean did you really think I gave away the motel across the street? And what about the shoe? Who would give out one shoe for a prize if it was a serious contest?"

He and his brother gave me dead pan looks. They thought I was kidding. "We came in first," the guy said, as if I was the one who didn't understand.

"It took me almost an hour to get here," the brother with the truck added, as if that work alone was deserving of a grand piano.

The discussion began to get heated, but in the end, there were more of us than there were of them. One of our roadies gave the winning brother a joint, and they seemed at least mollified by the time they left, sadly, without the piano.

"Geezus, what a couple of butt pokes," said Fritz, our lighting tech, who seemed quite entertained by the whole exchange. The next night when we arrived at the club, the manager was waiting for us.

"Someone called from the state attorney general's office. That guy who won the piano complained. You gotta be more careful about what you give away," he said sternly.

"Geezus, what a couple of butt pokes," said Fritz.

By the end of the year, we were playing five days a week almost every week and continually adding to our growing repertoire. There were a lot of gigs at college mixers at UMass in Amherst (affectionately known as ZooMass) and the morning after one show there, we were driving to get breakfast when the song 'I Don't Want to Grow Up' from the Broadway version of Peter Pan started playing in my head. Maybe I was hung over but I heard it up tempo and with pounding drums. We worked it out and played it that night and we've been playing it ever since.

By now in our career, the Rathskellar, or "The Rat" as everyone called it, was the new music center of Boston. Located in a dank, dark cellar in Kenmore Square, a baseball's throw from Fenway Park, it became ground zero for the growing punk scene that was beginning to thrive in The Hub. Our good friends, The Nervous Eaters, were one of the great bands that came out of that scene, as well as other soon to be Boston legends like Mission of Burma, and The Neighborhoods.

But it wasn't all about punk; on any given night, you could also see an excellent, straight ahead rock band like The Stompers lighting it up. We played The Rat once and hated it. There was a dark, desperate energy about the place that didn't appeal to me. I always thought that the owner couldn't have been more lucky that a stripped down, hardcore genre of music chose his dump to get born in.

It wasn't only that the place stunk, or that your feet stuck to whatever was left of the carpet. The toilets were often just, I swear to God, holes in the floor, and you could expect to be treated like crap from the moment you walked in. If there was an award for "Shithole Club of the Month," this place would have had a wall full of trophies.

The local rock press seemed to like the symmetry of this new stripped down style of music taking place in a foul, bad smelling dump. I wondered more than once how the writers would feel if instead of going back to their offices to write stories and reviews, they had to work at a place like The Rat. Maybe it wouldn't have seemed quite so romantic. Having said that, The Police played their first American show there. Tom Petty & The Heartbreakers, Thin Lizzy, The Ramones and The Talking Heads all played the Rat.

Bands like Mission of Burma could receive glowing accolades and be named "Beantown's best band" by *The Boston Globe*, and not be able to draw enough in the suburbs to afford playing there. For the most part, only The Neighborhoods, The Stompers, The Eaters, and The Del Fuegos, were able to leave that very insular scene and play outside of the Boston/ Cambridge area.

Rather than gig the Rat, audition at larger clubs like The Channel, or play the newly opened Paradise on an off night, we decided to stay out of Boston until it made sense and money. Not only could we make more money in the 'burbs, but our opportunities were greater. The Frolics in Salisbury, just south of the New Hampshire border, was a club that held over a thousand people, and we had the chance to back up different national and regional bands there.

Our show with renowned guitarist Rick Derringer there went well enough that we did a mini tour of New England with him. We also played The Frolics with Steppenwolf, one of the many touring versions of the band minus singer John Kay. It didn't matter to us; this was our first tiny taste of the Big Time. It was also the first time we'd seen a totally fucked up rocker at close hand.

Nick St. Nicholas, although a member of

Steppenwolf during its heyday, was fired by John Kay in 1970, and yet here he was seven years later with his own version of the band. An early sign that all wasn't well with Nick, happened at our afternoon sound check. I walked into the empty audience to listen to my band play an instrumental, and was soon joined by an apparently very drunk, stoned and bleary St. Nicholas.

"Iglabooba," he said.

"Huh?" I replied.

"Beesablabla drummer," he answered.

I realized then that he was talking about Chris, our drummer, but I wasn't sure what point he was trying to make. In a real life situation you would walk carefully away from loonies like this, but he was famous goddammit so he must have been trying to say something important to me.

It turned out, I think, that he thought Chris was a female, because he seemed to be asking me if the drummer was going with anyone. In his defense, we were well back from the stage, and even then, female drummers were not unheard of. Also, Chris had long blond hair. (the comedian in me wants to add: he also had a perfect ass, but he'd kill me if he read that). I'm not sure how I answered his question about my drummer, but he must have felt closure, because he stumbled away.

Later that night, after our opening set, he visited

our dressing room mumbling something about a bathroom. He then made it over to a sink that had no bottom attaching pipe, and peed into it, the urine covering his shoes below.

Satisfied, he said, "Balbalabba," and left.

I couldn't believe it possible that anyone that fucked up could play, never mind go on stage. As it turned out, it wasn't possible; during Steppenwolf's third song, St. Nicholas fell straight back into his amp and hit the deck. Rather than stopping the show, the band finished the song as if they were thinking, "oh fuck, here we go again." They got him to his feet between songs, he raised his fist like he'd done something cool, and the band finished the night.

It's odd to think how great success and notoriety can destroy some people, maybe all they ever wanted was to be in a band playing music with some friends, but then it got crazy. Money, stress, women, drugs; they can all bring it to an end, until you're playing in your own tribute band, and hoping no one calls you on the fact that the guy who sang and wrote all the songs isn't in the house. If it came to that, I think I'd rather haul hides in a leather factory.

CHAPTER SIX

John and Yoko were Fools' Fans?!

*"I'll do the stupid thing first, and then
you shy people follow."*
Frank Zappa

By the middle of 1977, our collegiate approach to rock had not only brought us to some regional prominence, but also attracted the attention of a fledgling, but first rate Boston booking agent named Tim Collins. We thought we were already playing a lot, but when Tim began booking us our calendar exploded. It wasn't that he was cracking a whip over us, I think he'd just finally found a local band that could play anywhere. His credo seemed to be that hard work was good for bands and that was fine with us.

In 1984, Tim went on to achieve what many at that time thought impossible: he brought the so-called "Toxic Twins" Steven Tyler and Joe Perry back together and reunited, and then managed Aerosmith to their rightful place as one of the premier bands on the planet. But for now, his goal was to get us Fools work, and that's what he did. A blues bar in Maine, a VFW in Rhode Island, an opera house in Lake Placid, it didn't matter to us; if Tim booked it we'd play it. Over the next six months, we played an astonishing one hundred and twenty-one shows in two hundred and twelve days, or sixty percent of the possible days available on the calendar. An impressive accomplishment despite nights where it seemed like getting on stage would be impossible.

Stacey broke his arm and played in a cast for a month (an amazing feat for a guitar player), Doug got laryngitis and couldn't speak above a Clint Eastwood whisper, and I played with a flu that had my temperature up to a hundred and three degrees and had me vomiting into a bucket behind the speakers during Rich's solos...as if his solos were the cause of my problems.

There were nights when we drove through blizzards and nights when somebody's vehicle broke down. But like carnie folk, no matter what happened, we somehow got to the next town, set up the equipment and were ready to do the show.

It's amazing what extended periods of playing in a band can do to your view of humankind, especially if you're in a so called "party band." You tend to see people at their most vibrant and extreme, and it's not all happy stuff. We liked to think that, in some form, we were bringing the circus to town, and along those lines, our audiences showed up expecting a certain amount of spectacle and were therefore louder, drunker, higher and more uninhibited than audiences of most other bands.

There were nights when naked women jumped on stage, and nights when motorcycles were driven onto the dance floor. Like any good rabble rouser, I began to develop a sense that the crowd was a single, large organism, and that allowed me to feed it, tickle it, taunt it or stroke it as the need dictated. If you do it correctly, your reward is an amazing amount of positive energy and it's directed right at you. It's almost like sex, minus the messy cleanup and the guilty promise of a phone call. Anyhow, whenever someone asks, "where do you guys get all that energy," my answer is simple; it comes from the audience.

Some nights, when it's all clicking, and the spirit moves you, literal magic happens. I've climbed ten foot high speaker stacks and then jumped up and out, something I wouldn't normally do for lots of money, to land in a crouch on the stage and not felt the slightest ache.

One sweaty summer night at a place called Grovers in Beverly, Massachusetts I jumped high in the air to end a song, not knowing that someone had left a glass beer mug at my feet. As I landed, I brought my hand down hard, and before it hit the stage the end of my middle finger hit the top of the beer mug and continued through to the floor. I thought I'd cut off the end of my finger, but when I looked down there was a perfect V-shaped piece missing from the glass where my now buzzing appendage had passed completely through it, like the finger of a Kung Fu master. The local rock scene in Boston was so intense at this time that I thought it was all quite normal. Everyone was probably doing parlor tricks or imitating Jet Li on stage.

The creation of a party on any given night became our job and we learned early on that it was not our role to join it. I was like a circus ringmaster that orchestrated the affair, but prohibited from entering any of the three rings. As Gino told us early on, "If you party too much with the audience, that's where you'll end up." The bodies of bands who didn't heed this advice litter the history of rock n roll and we were determined not to join them.

One of our more memorable early shows happened late in the summer of '77 at a field in Haverhill, and it was called Footestock. The brainchild of the enterprising Foote family from Ipswich, it had started in 1975 as a back yard beer and pot party with fifty people and a

Footestock '77 Crowd

couple of bands. In two short years it became the biggest summer party in greater Boston; an estimated five thousand people attended the event.

In the days before internet, texting and social networking, the show was promoted by posters, handbills, and word of mouth. It also didn't hurt that in the days leading up to the show a crew of loonies painted orange footprints on all of the major roadways north of Boston leading to the location.

That '77 show featured us, the soon to be signed Cars, and another good Boston band called Reddy  Teddy. The Cars showed up in a limo that slowly moved through the crowd taking them to the back of the stage. Years later, when Rich was playing in Cars' bass player Ben Orr's solo band, Ben told him that when they drove through the crowd that day, people thought they were The Fools and that the limo was a stunt. It was truly an example of how alive and kicking the local music scene was in the late seventies that such a 'wing and a prayer' event could happen and be such a smashing success.

By the end of that year, we were writing constantly and felt that we were ready for the next step. A lawyer friend of ours, Dino Brown, knew a woman who knew a guy who'd had some success managing bands. That guy was Peter Casperson, and his soon to be New York based company was called Castle Music. Peter looked and acted the part of a manager; suit and tie, nicely coifed hair and an intelligent and professional demeanor.

Long before he met us, he'd managed a one hit wonder from Boston called The Road Apples, and managed Jonathan Edwards (Sunshine) to a gold record. He'd also managed comedian and actor Martin Mull to national prominence. Though he seemed to have a good eye for talent, it was his one fatal flaw that it wasn't always that eye he used.

Not long after we signed with him, I passed an attractive blonde woman leaving his office and I asked him who she was. As I remember, Peter's response went something like this:

"She's into dance club music and wants me to get involved in her career. She sings pretty well and she's a hard worker, but I think I'm going to pass."

I later learned the woman's name was Madonna; yes, the very same Madonna who managed to sell more records in the twentieth century than any other woman in the world. Though Peter did well by us, a running band gag lasted long after our relationship with him ended. Whenever a new female star would show up on the horizon a dialog like this would ensue.

Mike: "What do ya' think of this Britney Spears kid? Should we sign her?"

Rich: "I don't know...she dresses like a slutty teenager...does anybody really like that?"

Mike: "Naah...nobody likes that."

In this same manner, our imaginary management company has also passed on Pink

(wrong color), Lady GaGa (stupid name) and Taylor Swift (good singer but too innocent...nobody likes that).

Despite his gaff with Madonna,

Post Peter make over shot

Post Peter Makeover Shot

Peter was soon at work trying to hone us into something nationally marketable. To this end, most of the few days we had off were spent in New York City. There were hairdressers to meet, clothing shops to explore and endless discussions on band direction. I happily traded in my thick glasses for contact lenses and it was decided that we needed a band "look" because we were a bit rough around the edges.

In retrospect, that roughness and our general irreverence were probably one of the most appealing things about us. The punk/new wave uniform of leather jackets and torn dungarees was at one end of the spectrum, and the Power Pop jacket and skinny tie uniform stood at the other. Because of the chances we took on stage, I felt emotionally closer to punk and its implied danger, but musically we were no doubt more pop than anything else. Trying to fit us into some form of recognizable product became "The Project."

At first we were tentative about being anything other than what we were, a grungy bunch of knuckleheads, but once the thought is put in your head that you need to make a change for the greater good, it starts to work on you. It was as if BIG TIME ROCK was a very select club that didn't allow just anyone in. I think Peter's dream was that we make it to the big arenas; that's of course where the big money is, and it would be a lie to say that we didn't eventually jump on board that vision. After all, which would you rather do: play the big shot on stage to twenty thousand people or, I don't know…let's say, work in a coalmine? (All you good people from Ipswich put your hands down; coal mining is not the correct answer.) Soon enough we started "looking like a band" instead of perhaps a bowling team or a moped biker gang.

Early in 1978, we released our first homemade single, a song called 'She Looks Alright in the Dark.' The cover of the 45 was a cartoon of a girl with a paper bag over her head. It was a celebration of all that is stupid in the lustful, young American male. The topic was fertile ground that we would return to more than once in our songs over the years.

So we had a record now, what next? Well, it's clearly no fun having a record out if a radio station doesn't play it, and to that end we began working on our promotional campaign. Since we had no money, and Peter was looking at this first single as more of a testing of the water, we were forced to rely on our own ingenuity to get any airplay at all. To this end, we

The band with Peter (far right)

came up with a form letter to send to radio stations, along with our single. It went something like this:

Dear (Sir, Madam, To Whom It May Concern),

We are big fans of your (radio station, TV show, newspaper) and hardly a day goes by when we don't (listen to, watch, read) it. Enclosed you will find a (record by us, a picture of us, a bag of money) that we hope you will enjoy. Please know that anything you can do to help us in our current endeavor will surely earn you (our undying devotion, a place in heaven, another bag of money). (yours truly, yours affectionately, yours for a price), THE FOOLS

The idea was that we would cross out two of every three choices...you get the idea.

This may not have seemed like the most prudent approach to some, but as Bob Dylan said "when you ain't got nothin' you got nothin' to lose."

The single and the elaborate promotional campaign went mostly (and deservedly) ignored except for two weekend Boston disc jockeys. The first was Leslie Palmiter, who had a most excellent Sunday night show on WCOZ called *The Boston Beat*, which focused on local music. The second was Edward Hyson, otherwise known as Oedipus, who also had a Sunday night show on WBCN, a show more geared towards punk and new wave.

It's hard to explain the joy that one feels upon hearing your song for the first time on the radio. It didn't matter that it sounded thin and poorly recorded, and that it was played at eleven p.m. on a Sunday night; it was us and we now officially existed! Oddly enough for so small a grain of recognition, after this, our fan base also walked with a certain strut. And it should be acknowledged that our previously mentioned back up date around this time with The Doobie Brothers in Portland, Maine was landed (to ours and Peter's credit) without any real airplay. We were all about the stories people told about us that soon became legend, and more importantly, we were a good band and we had a good manager.

So now we had to think about our follow up song and here's the story of how it came about...and it may or may not be true, but I think it is. I was hanging out in a bar playing pool with a friend of mine (now an airline pilot) named Ted Ciolek and, shockingly enough, we'd had a few beers. The song 'Psycho Killer' was playing and when the "fa fa fa fa" part came on, Ted started clucking. Were we talking about chickens or barnyard animals before the song came on? I don't really know, but for some reason it was funny. In place of the lyrics "Psycho killer, *qu'est ce que c'est*" I immediately heard the phrase "Psycho Chicken, what the fuck?" I'm not saying it was genius, but such is the power of beer. The big, stupid song was written within a week.

When it eventually got released, the big, stupid rock press would act as if it were our own personal rebellion against new wave music, instead of us doing what we do, which is have big, stupid fun. The odd thing was that, no matter how silly we thought our version of the song, it was at the expense of a band, and a song that I really liked.

Sure I thought David Byrne was a bit full of himself, but so are most of the icons of rock and it wasn't personal. I was told that, after people kept clucking during their performances of 'Psycho Killer,' The Talking Heads stopped playing the song. Who knew the power of a bad joke?

In the category of some things that never seem

to go away, to this very day I still get 'Psycho' royalty checks (however small) from such disparate places as Australia, France, Japan and Papua New Guinea (a place we've never toured but I'm assured we are HUGE there). While I do not hesitate to cash the checks, I would mostly agree with what I was told Byrne's response was to a question about our take on his tune. "It's a clever version of a brilliant song."

I would correct him and say, "it's a big, stupid version of a clever song."

By the end of that summer of 1978, we did two things that would make an impression in the calendars Rich was keeping at that time (which thankfully, he's kept to this day as a running record of every show, recording session, etc.). "Record 'Psycho Chicken'" is mentioned casually in the middle of October amidst all the gigs we were playing, but one other date stands out with exclamations.

The gig doesn't really matter, but under it is written: "with Gino!!" In a move that was both overdue and well needed we finally hired our old friend Gino away from his empty club to be our road manager. Throughout his time with us, Gino always put us at the top of the heap. "I don't work for Peter," he would say, "I work for you."

It was also around this time period that the band started to get more notice in the press. We were described as "madcap'" and "zany" and the things I did on stage were my "antics." Even now, thirty plus years later, at least one of those three words is sure to show up in almost any article written about us. Some writers included all three in a story. One writer, in an early story, hit the trifecta in a single line with this: "Zany lead singer Mike Girard continued his antics when he came out dressed in a trench coat and little else to lead The Fools through a madcap version of 'Mack the Knife.'" I don't know why but those three words have always made me feel like a hand puppet.

One night, in the fall of '78, Peter brought David Bieber to see us at a club in Newburyport. David was then a bona fide "man behind the scenes" at WBCN, and after hearing the crowd's response to the band, and 'Psycho Chicken,' he suggested that we send the station a tape of the song. It was a shot in the dark to send a tape out to a station, but the thinking was that it was cheaper than cutting a single, and we could always record it later if there was any identifiable response from the listening audience. The Cars had sent BCN a tape of 'Just What I Needed' the previous year and the response was so overwhelming that the band was signed to Elektra Records.

Ken Shelton had the midday show and at noon he always played something food related. Most of the songs were in house creations with titles like 'Only the Good Bye Lunch' and 'Only Bologna'. It seemed like a good place for a song about chicken. Ken played it and they received some listener calls asking about the song. You must remember that WBCN in 1978 was still all about the music, and they greatly respected audience input. A week later Charles Laquidara, the original legend at the seminal station, played it once a day as his Big Mattress Song of the Week.

Charles was the perfect person to introduce us to the listeners of greater Boston; like us he was childish, abrasive and charming; all at the same time. There was always the sense that Charles didn't really give a fuck if he got ratings; he was entertaining himself, and if you were also entertained as a listener, he was ok with that. Over the years, we would appear (if you can use that word for radio) on his morning show close to a dozen times, and though Charles would periodically have meltdowns during commercial breaks and fire and then rehire half of his staff, he always treated us like friends of the show. Whatever it is that we do, Charles always got it.

Within a week of the Mattress exposure the song was being played on all shifts and by the end of that month it was in heavy rotation (twenty to fifty plays a week). It was still just a tape when WCOZ, WAAF, WHEB, WHJY, and the other major stations in New England started playing it. We did a live December broadcast from The Summit Club in Peabody on WCOZ, the other big station in Boston and by Christmas time, still a tape, it was being played on FM stations in New York, San Francisco, and Houston, having been sent, in some cases, from one station to another.

We had a friggin' hit song, but still we weren't selling it. It was a little embarrassing to get equal or more airplay in certain towns than The Eagles or Rod Stewart, and not have anything to show for it. Was it bad management and Peter's thought that we should go for the big score, or was it more likely the almost paranoid feeling record companies have always had about novelty songs?

Had we found a way to distribute it nationally ourselves, then we could have gone ahead and made a single. But back then, only the major record companies could really get your records around and into the stores, and so we sought out a major record company deal.

It seemed like a foregone conclusion that someone would have wanted to sign us; all the legwork of breaking the song on major national stations was already done. We also had another twenty or so original songs ready to record, not all of them funny, but all with a certain bend. We recorded a sampling of these and, like eager schoolboys looking for a hot prom date, sent the demos around to all the hottest cheerleaders, um, excuse me, I meant major record labels. Atlantic, Epic, Capitol, EMI; the list went on. They all received a chance to pick up some easy cash on a song already well on its loony way around the country. We waited by the phone for the calls to start streaming in and then…nothing happened. It was like we had a bad connection or something; "HELLOOO!

IS THIS PHONE WORKING? HELLOOO!"

By January of '79, we played our first major (for us) Boston gig and sold out The Paradise on a snowy Wednesday night. Since that venue had hosted most of the soon to be major acts that came through New England, from The Police, to Elvis Costello to AC/DC, and many others, this was a big deal for us. For the first song,

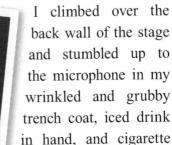

I climbed over the back wall of the stage and stumbled up to the microphone in my wrinkled and grubby trench coat, iced drink in hand, and cigarette hanging from my lip and Doug introduced me as Don Law.

At that time, Law was already well on his way to becoming the most powerful rock promoter, club owner, and entrepreneur on the East Coast. He also seemed to have an almost Howard Hughes like persona about him in that he avoided the spotlight. I mumbled something to the audience about how they were "the salt of the earth" and how it was "the little people" like them who made my life as a power broker so much fun. Then I sang 'Mack the Knife,' did a pratfall spilling my drink, and crawled backstage to quickly change clothes and emerge as me, Mike Girard. The next day one of the Boston papers called it madcap, and mentioned how gutsy we were to lampoon Don Law. We didn't feel that it took any guts whatsoever, as he was so far above our station in life as to be untouchable. Think of ants bothering an elephant; it probably doesn't happen.

By now we were starting to have the uneasy feeling that the prom was getting closer and still we had no date. Since all the hot chicks had refused us, we started thinking about the less attractive record labels in hopes that they had a good personality. To that end we started courting them, most of whose names I forget, thinking that they might be enticed to "go all the way."

Unfortunately, they were no kinder than the babes. Many of them had the feel of our promotional form letter:

Dear (Insert Band Name Here),

Thank you for sending us your (record, picture, bag of money) and thinking of us, but we are not interested.

Sincerely, (Record Label Name)

The unspoken words were probably more like this:

Dear Band,

We don't want you. Next time try to write some hit songs and quit trying to be such a bunch of funny assholes.

The one rejection notice I do remember clearly was more for its irony than anything else. A label called Planet Records told us that we weren't "universal" enough. I thought jeez neither are you or your name would be Universal Records.

After a few frustrating months, 'Psycho' quieted down, the prom came and went, and we were left, boner in hand, to wonder what the fuck just happened?

Now, rather than sit still and rot on the vine, we decided to take action, and like a bunch of six year olds who can't believe that people don't think that they're cute and wonderful, we performed our trick again. We sent out a tape of 'It's a Night for Beautiful Girls' to stations who'd played 'Psycho,' and sure enough, most of them played it and it went to heavy airplay in many of the same markets.

By now, we weren't the only ones who were confused. Some of the non-New England stations seemed uncomfortable with a band that kept giving out its product for free and carefully backed away from us, as if our libertine conduct with our affairs might infect them and the whole industry. We actually ended up being ahead of the curve as in time just such a thing would happen to the industry, and when it did, it was long overdue.

Undeterred by our lack of label dating success we played another fifty out of ninety nights from January to March in places like Albany, Worcester,

Providence and Montreal. One night in particular leaps out in Rich's calendars; March 4th (1979) which said this: WBCN STRIKE BENEFIT, ORPHEUM BOSTON.

Why would the most successful radio station in America at the time need a benefit you ask? It seems that Michael Wiener, as the head of Hemisphere Broadcasting Corporation, bought the station and like a true "suit" decided it was overstaffed and fired nineteen of the thirty-six beans he counted.

This hit Boston like a kick in the balls; the station had become an institution and people rallied to the news that Local 262 had voted to strike in favor of the terminated employees. The station had such swag with the town and the surrounding communities that the moment an Orpheum concert was mentioned to benefit the fired workers, you either wanted to play it or go to it.

We of course landed on the play side of things and got to do a couple of tunes that night along with The J. Geils Band and other local favorite Robin Lane & The Chartbusters. In some ways, it may have been the last great coming together of the music community in Boston. One of the people let go by the station was Oedipus, one of the first to ever play us, and a shining light for what would eventually become known as alternative music. The strike and ensuing benefit caused a rethinking by Wiener and company and also a realization by many that big business was always lurking around the edges of any good thing, ready to repackage, reprogram and dumb down a concept to its often least attractive, but most mass marketable product.

By 1981 Oedipus would ironically become the program director, proving that some people are not good judges on the quality of "beans." Years later in the mid-nineties, 'BCN would fall victim to its own success and become the epitome of corporate rock which eventually lead to its demise. On August 12, 2009, the station that had greatly supported us and was credited with introducing U2 to America went silent after forty-one years on air.

April 1st of 1978, our national holiday, saw us back at The Paradise for a live 'BCN broadcast. One thing of note happened that night. In the week leading up to the show, John and Yoko were seen about town and there were rumors that they were interested in relocating to Boston. On our guest list that night were two good friends from Ipswich, Walter and Lucille Fedrocki, an older couple who'd more than once offered us their cellar as a place to rehearse. Walter was a slightly built, balding man with glasses and a great sense of humor, and Lucille was taller, larger and every bit as jovial.

We'd asked them earlier in the day to dress up like rock stars, and they did the best they could; Walter in skinny tie and jacket, and Lucille in shiny dress and wrap around fur. At some point in the show

I made reference to the Lennons being in the area and said that we had a big surprise. Then I asked Walter and Lucille to stand up, and introduced them as "John Lennon and Yoko Ono!"

The people at The Paradise laughed, clapped, and cheered, as if they felt happy to be in on the joke, and the people listening at home could only believe that the famous couple was in the house. Time changes all stories and this one has become legend in that many people have seriously told me they were there the night John and Yoko came to see The Fools. Oh that it were true!

In May, we played the legendary CBGB in New York for the first time and found it to be every bit the shithole that The Rat in Boston was. But it was from that pile of shit that beautiful roses grew like Patti Smith, The Ramones, Blondie, The Talking Heads and many others. Knowing we would be in the city, we rented a rehearsal hall and invited all of the dozen or so major labels to what was then called a showcase.

What it meant was you get up on a stage with sound and lights and play your songs to a group of record execs who sit at separate tables in the dark like lonely weirdoes in a porno movie theater, none of them clapping, smiling or acknowledging the others' existence. Amongst those attending of note, was Andrew Loog Oldham, who had managed the Rolling Stones back in the sixties.

We set up a bar and hired a woman to bring drinks to these jerkoffs and once they were a bit liquored up, we played seven or eight songs, minus the now fear inspiring 'Psycho Chicken.' Silence followed every song, and so, like a man who can't handle a vacuum, I started to babble in between songs, saying things like "don't forget to tip your waitress" and "how about those Yankees?" and "do any women come to this club?" The suits were not amused; they listened to our songs, drank our booze and exited the hall without so much as a cursory nod. Peter said that it was the standard practice of these gatekeepers that they not show their cards to each other but I left thinking "what a perfect job to have if you're an asshole."

With everything that went on that month we still found the time to play twenty shows in thirty-one days, which was a good thing considering what the showcase cost us. June came and we had two weeks off but still played fifteen shows, the crowner of which was June 29th with Blondie at the Orpheum in Boston. We had a great show in front of our hometown crowd and even got an encore, something unheard of for an unsigned opener.

I was standing back stage next to 'BCN DJ Marc Parenteau during Blondie's set when a young EMI exec named Gary Gersh walked by. We'd met Gary once before and he seemed like a straight shooter. Marc said something to him like "Why the fuck don't you guys sign The Fools, what's wrong with you?"

The next day two things happened; first there was an article in *The Globe* about the show written by my favorite rock writer, Steve Morse. He said that we "opened the show on an uproarious and musically stunning note." He also said we had a "levitating intensity" and that we "got by on more than novelty." He then mentioned that we were a "zany North Shore group," but for him, one out of three of the infamous trifecta was forgivable.

Second, we found out that Gersh had recommended that EMI sign us as soon as possible. After years of struggling, giving away our music, playing wherever and whenever we could and having very little to show for it, we'd finally done it. The Fools, those crazy lads from a small coal mining town called Ipswich, were going to what we considered the big-time.

The real craziness was about to begin.

CHAPTER SEVEN

Send in the clowns…and the monkey!

"It was like some Roman orgy. Everyone was totally drunk, there were naked people on the lawn, and this fucking monkey was running around shitting and biting people. I still can't believe anyone ever let them in that place."

Anonymous woman remembering The Fools'
Castle Hill "We got signed" party

It all started innocently enough; we wanted to celebrate the fact that we'd just gotten signed to a major label. This was big news in our town. John Updike had long since strip mined the available local stories and moved away, and aside from the odd enormous clam dug up on the clam flats, the town didn't have that much to brag about.

Looking back, it's hard to describe the impact our signing had on the town of Ipswich and more importantly, on us. We'd always had an admittedly working class appeal, and it would be no crime of exaggeration to call our humor lowbrow, but this was one time when we would attempt to take the high road and have a big classy party. This was going to be our chance to stay connected to "our people" and let them revel in our moment of triumph. On the other hand, it was a way for us to cover our asses so that when we left town on our way to the big time, no one would get to say we had changed.

Since our goal was to make this event free of charge to the public, the first order of business was to choose a site big enough that could hold lots of people and also allow us to perform. There was only one place in Ipswich that fit that description; the mansion at The Crane Estate at Castle Hill. If you've ever seen the movie *The Witches of Eastwick*, much of it was filmed here; it was the enormous house that Jack Nicholson's devil character lived in.

Built in 1928 on a hill overlooking the Atlantic Ocean by Richard T. Crane Junior, it's a beautiful fifty-nine room Stuart style English mansion. Much of it was removed from a real British mansion, boxed, and shipped to Ipswich for its re-creation. You've seen the Crane name before, but given the nature of our human plumbing, probably more men recognize the name than women. It's a name that has adorned many a toilet, as Crane's Chicago based plumbing company made millions from the development and sale of the first mass produced plumbing parts and flush toilets.

Crane was a plumbing magnate (word meaning "great man" in Latin) who became a tycoon and played in some of the same circles as Andrew Carnegie and John D. Rockefeller, but considering where his money came from, there must have been some giggles at any function when he arrived. Looking back, I now realize that, aside from it being logistically perfect for us, it was also ironically perfect. It wouldn't matter how much money he ever made, or how well he was educated, even if he could write and speak classical Greek (which he couldn't), Richard T. Crane was still a guy who made toilets. To the other famous captains of industry who came from steel and oil he must have seemed uncultured in comparison.

Once we had targeted the place as our celebration party location, the next step was to convince whoever was in charge to let us rent the joint for the night. We knew it was available for a price, as they often had jazz concerts, lavish wedding receptions and fittingly enough, chamber music. Although Peter was very skeptical of the need for such a party, thinking that the money to make it happen could be used in other areas, he was also the perfect point man for this endeavor.

So it was that we made an appointment, showed up at the allotted time, and were met at the front door of the mansion by an attractive, but stern looking woman named Olga, who managed the functions for the estate. Olga was tall, blonde, hair worn in a bun, black dress, horn rimmed glasses and gave off the unmistakable whiff of culture and good breeding. The Cranes had long since disappeared from Ipswich and the mansion and surrounding 2100 acres were managed by a group of trustees; Olga was the gatekeeper we had to get by in order to have our bash.

Peter had made the call setting up the meeting, and his extended hand and warm, tooth filled smile, seemed to distract Olga from the five scruffy men accompanying him. While she and Peter talked, we Fools scurried around checking the place out. Even though we'd grown up in Ipswich, this was our first glimpse of the inside of the mansion. We weren't disappointed; beautiful paneled walls, parquet floors, a library with ornate carvings and a grand piano at the foot of a grand staircase gave the mansion all the drama and pageantry appropriate for our upcoming festivity.

Upon seeing the interior, a plan quickly developed; Rich thought that the best room for us to play in would be the dining room. It supposedly held about a hundred people seated, so we figured we could jam in about two hundred standing. That meant we would probably play two shows, one at nine and one at eleven, giving everyone attending a chance to see us. We also hatched a plan to give the event a circus atmosphere with jugglers, mimes, clowns and whatever else we could patch together.

To top it off, Chris said he knew a guy who owned a monkey that wore a little round hat and would do tricks (the monkey, not the guy). My brother John had been quite a talented mime during the Great Mime Scare of the mid-seventies and though he had since moved on to acting (short factoid; John would later appear in the *Smugglers Blues* episode of *Miami Vice* and kill Glenn Frey's character at the end), he knew some people who could help flesh out our dream.

Before we left, one final scheme was hatched; we decided that we would give away some money. The thought was that we would take five hundred one dollar bills, and place them individually inside of five hundred balloons. Then we'd fill the balloons with helium, attach each to a long string and release them to float up to the twenty five foot high ceiling. People would pull the balloons down by the string, pop them, and find the money. Peter was aghast at this last idea. It went against everything he'd learned in business school.

"Why would you want to give money away?" he asked.

"It'll give the whole night a crowning touch," I explained, "and it's like we're giving back something real to our fans. Plus there's something about it that's funny; you know like, pull the string, pop a balloon, and get a dollar."

Peter wasn't seeing the genius of it.

"Yeah," Doug added, "and when people realize there's money in the balloons, it'll be like a gold rush stampede. It'll be great!"

Peter didn't think that the idea of a gold rush stampede in a crowded building was a good idea either, but he grudgingly agreed to the plan as long as we didn't make a formal announcement about the balloon money during our shows.

"Let people discover it for themselves," he said.

He also told us that Olga would only agree to this rock 'n roll party if it was done by invitation only. This last condition fell in line with Peter's idea that the party would give him a chance to invite certain Boston area media types and Olga's condition would also keep the riffraff to a minimum. The mistake made here was trying to ignore the fact that our fan base was essentially made up of the same riffraff that Olga and Peter wanted to keep out of the party. We settled on the idea that we'd invite about a hundred of our most hardcore fans and the other hundred or so guests would be at Peter's discretion.

Over the course of the next few weeks, we lined up a stage, hired a caterer, had the invitations printed and sent and met with various talented "extras." My brother introduced us to a few people who seemed perfect for our idea of pomp and spectacle. They included an excellent three man juggling group, a piano player, an actress who could sing songs in German, an actor who did an excellent English accent and a mime or two thrown in for good measure. We also met a stoner from Newburyport named Fred who had a cute little monkey named Willy who would dance and bow when Fred sang the Happy Birthday song.

At the last minute we decided to add one more act; two guys who we called The Flying Zucchini Brothers. We'd met them during a sound check at a local club where they worked the bar and they showed us an amazing trick they could do. Barney would take a firecracker, light it, stand sideways, and put it quickly between his lips. Jimmy, standing ten feet away, would shoot out the fuse with an elastic before it went off. That same night we talked them into doing it on stage, they did, and the audience loved it. Now that our show roster was complete, we could step back, relax and anticipate a great evening.

This is how we planned on our sideshow acts as they'd interact with our party guests. The first thing you would see when you entered The Mansion was a pretty blond woman with heavy makeup and bright red lips, wearing a black slinky dress and draped across the grand piano at the foot of the stairs, singing love songs in German. Playing the piano dramatically, and with way too many flourishes, would be a handsome lad in a tuxedo. We thought this was funny.

The next thing you might encounter as you strolled around the place was a mime, maybe trying to escape from an invisible box, or pulling an imaginary rope, and trying to get you to help. When you didn't get involved enough, the mime would say, "Come on will you give me a hand here!" We thought this too was funny.

Another extra walking through the crowd would be a tall man, with a big mustache, wearing a wrinkled, cream colored suit and a pith helmet. His job was to walk up to people attending, and in a perfect British accent say things like, "Ripping good show eh?" We thought that this was absolutely fucking hysterical.

The three man team of jugglers was like an opening act; since they were so good, we would put them on in the big room just before each of our shows. We thought this was cool.

The Zucchinis would be brought on once halfway through our second show. We thought this was stupid, but still funny. Fred and his monkey, Willy, would wander through the crowd and do whatever they wanted. After all, everyone likes monkeys. We were sure about this one. Hindsight being what it is... maybe the monkey was a bad idea.

The first thing that went wrong was underestimating the degree to which our fans would go to crash what was essentially a private party. They just knew that a band that they'd seen play Footestock, a band that they'd watched come up through the ranks, a band that friggin' John and Yoko had come to see; there was no way that The Fools didn't want them at the party. It didn't matter that they were turned away at the gated front entrance; they parked their cars at the beach a half mile away and walked up through the woods. By halfway through the night, so many people had crashed the party through the woods that the guard at the gate gave up and let everyone else drive in.

Our dressing room for the night was a gorgeous bedroom on the second floor, complete with carvings, paneling and of course, a wonderfully appointed bathroom, so we were initially oblivious to the onslaught of extra guests. Soon enough though the stories of the budding Roman bacchanal filtered upstairs.

Chris had wandered downstairs and came back up to say, "The place is fucking packed! And somebody must have passed out some acid because it's getting really trippy down there."

Then Peter came in, dressed elegantly, and smiling way too much…when Peter smiled too much you knew he had some bad news. I wish I had played poker with him back then; I would have made some serious money.

"Was the monkey your idea?" he asked, smiling and walking past me without waiting for the answer.

"Monkey, what monkey?" I answered smartly, but I had a sinking feeling.

"The fucking monkey who's flying around the room, shitting on the food and shitting all over the people! And where did all these fucking people come from?" Peter asked, as if the North Shore of Boston was sparsely populated.

Our manager almost never swore, and his idea of raising his voice was to enunciate words more clearly, so I could tell he was really upset.

"Why don't I go down and take a look," I said, as if my viewing of the flying, shitting monkey and all the extra people would make everything okay. Peter's smile grew to impossible proportions in relation to his face, and he left the room quickly.

My first view of the event from the top of the stairs was unnerving, but special. First of all, there were way too many people in attendance. Like the Visigoths sacking Rome, our fans had burst through the doors, gobbled up all the food and were now moving through the place and having their way with our extras. Our tuxedoed piano player was standing, pushed by the mob up close to the piano, but like a true professional, he'd given up playing dirge-like German love songs; he was trying to play 'Great Balls of Fire,' the barrelhouse Jerry Lee Lewis classic.

Not to be outdone, our blond torch singer was standing on the piano, belting out the song in German.

Sadly, one of our poor mimes had taken refuge behind the piano and was either violently throwing up or doing an excellent impression of it. And over the whole people packed hall entryway scene, the monkey was making huge leaps; from priceless hanging painting to precious carved bookcase to antique chandelier, all the while making a high pitched squealing sound. In some ways it must have looked like a believers' view of the final days of man.

"Cool," Rich said, as the monkey made an impossible leap, grabbed a railing, and shot past us to enter the relative peace of the second floor. Fred was nowhere to be seen. Not knowing what to do, I pushed through the crowd and did what I always did back then when things got out of control; I went to find Gino.

He was having a smoke on the back veranda, watching people wander across the perfectly manicured lawn. We'd given him the night off, and barring any band safety issues, he was content to watch the chaos from a distance. Standing next to him, our other mime was taking a break from the action to have an imaginary smoke.

"You should quit," Gino said to the mime, "it's bad for you." The mime went into an imaginary coughing fit and finished by grinding his "smoke" out with his foot.

"Gino," I said, "what the fuck are we gonna do? There are too many people here."

Gino stubbed his cigarette out in a potted plant, folded his big arms across his chest and said with a smile, "What are you talking about? This is great. These are your people."

A drunken group of partiers was now climbing the statues that bordered the back lawn. One guy was doing a good impression of humping one of the naked female statues from behind, much to the delight of his friends. The mime was outraged. Years later I would find out that a young drummer named Leo Black was among those people partying on the lawn.

"But Peter's freaking out and that monkey is running wild," I said, watching a car pull onto the lawn to park.

"Fuck Peter," Gino said, "and the monkey will calm down. You better go with the flow, or this thing could get ugly."

He was right as always, although I didn't see how it could get much uglier. But it had gone too far now to stop, not without the help of many law enforcement types, dogs and tear gas. We'd neglected to hire a cop for the night, deciding to use some friends to take invitations at the door. There was nothing to do now but to ride this crazy wave to the shore.

"Maybe you guys should go on a little early," Gino remarked as we worked our way through the crowded rooms to the stage. When I took a mental step back from the whole mess and saw it for what it was, I realized that it was great; the building was bursting with energy and the people in it were having a blast.

On the way to the stage, I passed Peter trying to comfort a tearful Olga, his hand on her shoulder. I heard her say to him, "You never said there'd be a monkey."

"I know," Peter replied, patting her shoulder. "I know."

Since there was no room anywhere inside, the jugglers went to a well lit outside patio and put on a wonderful show to an appreciative audience. It was the coolest thing ever to watch them do their juggles under a clear night sky. After they finished, we were on our way to the stage in the dining room, when Stacey met me and said, "Maybe the Zucchinis should come up in the first set instead of the second set; they're really drunk."

At this point, it would take too long to get from

our upstairs room to the dining room, so we turned a large closet behind the stage into our pre-show dressing room. I could hear Doug in there laughing loudly. I entered to see The Flying Zucchini Brothers as I'd never seen them before.

In honor of tonight's show, they'd made costumes. Barney and Jim were each wearing purple tights, Zorro masks, and long sleeved, shiny yellow jerseys with the letters *FZB* emblazoned in black on the front. The crotches of their purple tights were bulging where they'd each lodged a large zucchini. They looked ridiculously awesome.

As soon as they saw me they jumped up and went into a three second spin and hop that ended with them down on one knee and their arms extended. This was gonna be great! Then they started talking and I realized Stacey was right; they were absolutely hammered.

"Maybe after this we'll tour with you guys," Jim said, sucking on a beer.

"Fucking right!" Barney yelled, or "the target" as Jimmy called him. Barney was doing shots of Jack.

"Okay, let's go on," Rich called and so we did. I don't remember much about the show, other than the place was packed and people were digging it. I do remember what happened when the Zucchinis came up. Halfway through the set I introduced them to the audience. The crowd went crazy as the two lads came up on stage, posing and strutting like they were from the World Wrestling Federation. Jimmy had the kind of tall, athletic build that could look good in almost any outfit. Barney, on the other hand, had a build like, well…Barney Rubble, and he was not entirely fitting into either the tights or the long sleeved jersey. There were bare, fleshy parts of him hanging out around the middle that only a mother could love.

The moment of truth arrived, they went to separate ends of the stage and Chris began a drum roll. I'd seen them do this trick many times and they'd never failed to pull it off. Tonight however Barney was swaying a little as he readied to light the firecracker, and Jimmy was blinking his eyes and squinting, as if he wasn't really getting a good view of things. Barney then lit the firecracker, put his hands behind his back, stuck his chin out and Jimmy gave his elastic a pull and calmly shot the firecracker out of Barney's mouth. The fact that it exploded off stage and the noise was drowned out by the cheering fans didn't matter to The Brothers; that wasn't how the trick was supposed to go. Jimmy was supposed to shoot the fuse out with the elastic. I was narrating the whole thing over the microphone and so I acted like they did what they were supposed to do. Jimmy would have none of it.

"Nope, nope, nope, we gotta do it again," he said waving his arms to the confused crowd and under his breath to Barney he added, "quit fucking moving."

"I'm not fucking moving," his partner muttered.

I was beginning to wonder if these boys hadn't sampled some of the acid that was rumored to be about. They took their places again and Chris began another drum roll, while I explained to the audience that this trick was even better than they thought it was, "He's going to shoot the fuse out of the firecracker."

The audience got very quiet, Barney did his thing, and Jimmy's shot went a quarter inch under the lit fuse. This had only happened once before, and that's why Jimmy kept a second elastic hanging on his finger. As the fuse burned down, Barney squeezed his eyes shut and made a whimpering sound while trying to extend his lips as far as he could from his face. Two things then happened in a split second: Jimmy's second shot hit Barney on the lips, and Barney instantly tried to spit out the firecracker. He almost succeeded; but it was probably still an inch from his lower lip when it went off.

There was an audible groan from the audience. Jimmy swore loudly and Barney was shaking his head like someone who'd been punched. I had the sudden horrible thought that Jimmy would keep demanding another try until Barney was either crippled or blind. I said something inane like, "that's okay folks, that's why we call them The Flying Zucchini Brothers! Let's hear it!" The audience clapped, the boys realized they were done, and they walked off swearing at each for Rich and since he'd been listening to Bob Marley, he put a reggae feel to it and turned it instantly into a pop tune.

We seemed to be able to complement each other's music; one of us coming up with the bridge, chorus or verse to the other one's tune. 'Spent the Rent' followed, and then 'College Girl.' One night I dreamed that we were playing a song on stage, and I woke up remembering only the first verse. Doug and I fleshed it out and the song 'Night Out' from our first album came from that dream. Rich and Stacey added solos and rhythms that brought our tunes to the finish point. Rich has always been a supreme technician; his solos go to the right place and he never overplays.

Stacey has a great feel for rhythm, as exemplified by his counter point strumming on 'It's a Night.' Chris was our Charley Watts, straight ahead and right on time, no matter what genre of music we delved into.

Stage characters started to develop. Aside from the army guy in 'WWII', there was Bobby Herring, a washed out, drunken, pervert in a trench coat, who sang 'Mac the Knife.' There was also a country guy in a cowboy hat who sang 'Johnny Yuma.' Within a few years, his name would become Mel Smith.

People started following us from place to place and as long as we stayed in our own area, on most nights we could look out at familiar faces.

Along with our budding success however there

other. Richie blasted into the start of another song, and we did our best to erase the crowd's memory of what had just happened.

We finished the set, yelled out that we'd be back in an hour, and just before we left the stage, I reached out over the crowd and grabbed one of the balloon strings. I pulled it down, popped the balloon, and held up a dollar for all to see.

Technically, this was not going against Peter's demand that we not announce the balloon money from the stage, but it didn't seem to matter. The crowd had seen amazing jugglers, talented actors, trick shots, and comical characters wandering the place all night; the fact that I had just made a dollar bill magically appear out of a balloon was only more eye candy for them. They clapped loudly and ignored the balloons.

When we got back to our room backstage, Jimmy and Barney were sitting across from each other, passing a bottle of Jack Daniels back and forth. They were still dressed in their costumes, right down to the Zorro masks, but the zucchinis were lying on a table. They weren't happy; Barney's lower lip had swollen to twice its size, and he was saying something to Jimmy that might have been, "Look what you did to my fucking lip!" It was hard to understand him; imagine trying to talk with a dinner plate stapled to your lower lip. But Jimmy would only take some of the blame.

"Maybe I should have stretched out the elastics

a little more, but god damn it, Barney, you were swaying, you know you were."

In order to keep the Jack from dripping out of his mouth, Barney had to keep his head back while he swallowed. Barney then slowly shook his head and said carefully, but miserably, "We should have brought some fucking clothes to change into."

Thinking about it earlier in the day, they must have envisioned walking among the masses in all their post-performance glory, accepting congratulations, and maybe even movie offers, but now they were left to hide back here, drink whiskey and think about what might have been.

It's amazing that when the night ended a few hours later, nothing was broken or stolen. Yes there were car track ruts on part of the lawn, and yes there were some naked people at one point frolicking near the naked statues. And yes, the police did show up after most everyone had gone, responding to a call that a monkey had bitten someone, but I later heard that it resulted from that person pulling Willy's tail. And since when the cops arrived, Fred was holding

a very docile and exhausted Willy, nothing came of the charge.

By about one in the morning, there were only the band,

the roadies and a few friends left in the mansion. Peter had spent most of the night trying to keep Olga from freaking out and doing something rash; like calling in the National Guard. He looked totally spent sitting on the steps of the grand staircase, a now drunk and giddy Olga, looking like a plane crash survivor, at his side.

The room that we'd played in was a mess; empty beer cups, paper plates, and crumpled up invitations covered the floor. Oddly enough, our one true act of generosity, the money balloons remained mostly untouched, some of them floating halfway down from the high ceiling. By the end of the second set, I'd gone so far as to tell the audience, plainly and clearly, that there was money in the balloons, but most people just laughed. Why would anyone put money in a balloon?

Ginny had spent a good part of the afternoon helping put money in the balloons, fill them with helium, and tie strings to them. She and I now sat on the front of the stage and watched Jimmy and Barney wander around the hall, like two dazed cartoon characters, but friends again, popping balloons and collecting dollars. As far as I know, they never did their trick again in public, if at all. People still mention them to me though all these years later, except with the happy ending of them performing the trick flawlessly. It's funny how people are, they want the story to turn out right, no matter the facts.

The event was over and in some ways more of a success than we'd ever imagined. The next day, the only mention of the party in the local paper had to do with police responding to a "wild monkey attack," as if such things occurred in New England. We've had many parties of note over the years, some of them almost as crazy, but the party at Crane's Castle was one of a kind.

CHAPTER EIGHT

Behold, the weird sponge!

*"Thank god for The Fools, the local boys made good, who
opened with an honest and upbeat show that exposed
The Knack for what they were-imposters."*

Steve Morse, Boston Globe, 11/12/79

We didn't agree with everything Steve Morse
said; yes we were honest and upbeat (I blush), and we
were local boys making good, but The Knack were
a first rate American pop band, and unless you're
allergic to that, it was nothing to be sneezed at.

It was an odd world we entered when we toured
with them. Our little band had just gotten signed that
summer with EMI, we were still a few months away
from recording our first album and yet through some
excellent high level work by Peter, here we were on
a national tour with the hottest young group
in America.

Yes, there were Eagles and Doobies, Pink Floyds
and Pretenders, Police, Clash, and Michael Jackson...
but only The Knack had a number one song for six
straight weeks that also became the end of the year
number one song on the all-important Billboard
charts. Anyone who was alive in the summer of
seventy-nine knows that you couldn't go anywhere
without hearing the song 'My Sharona' that lead

singer Doug Fieger wrote about his seventeen year old girlfriend Sharona Alperin. Her picture on the cover of that same single, looking like a Key West wet t-shirt winner, did nothing to thwart the sales of the record. And yet, The Knack did everything they could, intentionally or not, to piss off every radio station and newspaper in America.

Since they were Beatles freaks, they set up their stage presentation and gear to emulate the Fab Four; they dressed in black and white and they would even bow in unison at the end of their show. This seemed to infuriate the purists, but the thing that really set the media in general on edge was the band's idea that they would do very few radio and press interviews. It was customary back then for even the biggest rock stars to occasionally make the rounds of the FM stations, if not to promote a show, then at least to rub elbows with the people who were playing their music.

The Knack's decision of limiting this access at first seemed to lend an aura of mystery to the band, and the few press conferences held were well attended. But as the song climbed the charts in spite of the band's refusal to play nice with the media, the backlash began. It was as if the petulant radio and newspaper types were saying, "Now wait just a fucking minute, we are the king makers! Who do you little pricks think you're dealing with here!?" The "Nuke The Knack" campaign had begun and we had a front row seat to the action.

Once the lines were drawn between The Knack and the media, we became the only outlet for many a frustrated local entertainment writer. More often than not, as we crossed the country, we ended up doing the radio and press interviews that should have gone to The Knack. The reviews of the shows couldn't have gone much better for us; we were called "bouncing, fresh and entertaining" by a Miami newspaper. *The Fort Lauderdale News* said our set was "the brightest moment of the night" and that we were "loaded with energy and style." *The Detroit News* said that we were "sparkling and uninfected," which must have been good news to those people in closest contact with us.

Nowhere in any of the reviews did the words "madcap," "zany" or "antics" appear, probably because a thirty minute opening set doesn't allow much opportunity for shenanigans, but also because I think Peter was trying to hone us into an arena act.

Big time arena acts show up in your town, say the same things to you that they said the night before to a different town and hopefully plug in your town's name in the appropriate slot. Think of it more as a scripted musical, with all of the spontaneity and dynamics of professional wrestling. The fact is that we as a band on the Knack tour saw this experience in a different way; this time you'll get to hear our songs, but next time you'll get to see our show.

Through it all we had a ball, because while The Knack were aloof and distant to the press, back stage and behind the scenes they couldn't have been nicer to us. We got sound checks, hot meals, and the general feeling that we were all in this together. While Doug Fieger and young Sharona didn't hang out much, perhaps wanting to stay one step ahead of the Mann Act, the band's amazing drummer Bruce Gary was a good dude who liked to get out and see the sights.

One night he took Rich and me to a club on Chicago's South Side to see blues great Albert Collins. During the break between sets we went back stage to say hello and Albert greeted Bruce like a long lost friend, which is just what he was. Bruce hadn't told us on the way to the club that he'd toured with Albert prior to joining The Knack. Albert brought him up to play a few tunes in the second set and never mentioned the Knack thing to the crowd; this was just him bringing up a former well liked band mate. My already high opinion of Bruce soared. During our entire time on that tour, he was always willing to hang a little and talk to us; the opening act.

Since he hadn't written any songs, Bruce never made much money from The Knack, but when it ended a year or so later, rather than slip into obscurity, his career blossomed. He did studio work with giants like Bob Dylan, George Harrison and Stephen Stills, just to name a few. We couldn't have been happier for the guy. Of all of the members of The Knack, he seemed to most be deserving.

While on that tour, we had our first encounter with some of EMI's company representatives, otherwise known as record reps. These are the people in any given town who work on your record locally; the real foot soldier types who get the stations to play it, and make sure it's in all of the retail stores. Some of these people are really good at what they do, but like most professions, some of them really suck.

We were somewhere in the Midwest, another night, another successful show. We were grazing from a deli platter after our set, when a local rep called Dave came barging unannounced into our dressing room. Dave was middle-aged, a fleshy frame stuffed into an oversized baseball shirt and sporting a long pony tail; he looked like a hippie gone to seed.

"Okay, the first thing we gotta do is change your name," he said loudly to the room in general as he entered. "You don't have anything out yet, so it's not too late."

As I was the closest to him, Dave walked towards me with his hand extended. He had the lazy, loud, confidence of a guy who'd been the mayor of a small town for a long time. Like a true bureaucrat, he felt he would have his EMI job long after our little party bus left town, but first, we would be the unsolicited beneficiaries of his wisdom.

"I missed your show, how'd it go?" he asked,

shaking my hand. He didn't wait for an answer before spouting off again. "Seriously, who the fuck named you guys The Fools?"

He took a beer out of the ice bucket, chugged half of it and as he talked he would stop in front of each band member, grab that person's hand and shake it firmly. Gino watched with amusement from the other side of the room, as if it were a TV show.

"I'll tell you what I tell every new band that comes through here," he said, annoying anyone in earshot. "You do your job and make good music, and I'll do my job and try to get it played. I'll tell you the clubs you should play at and the people you should meet. That way we'll take over this market *excrementally*." I think he meant incrementally; a little at a time, but then again maybe he was warning us about the shitty job he would eventually do.

Doug was last in line and was still more interested in making a sandwich than he was in listening to Dave. The record company rep talked at Doug's back waiting for him to finish putting his sandwich together.

"You can't expect us local guys to help you if your record is crap. We can't make chicken soup out of chicken shit," he rambled on.

At this point, Doug turned around, his right hand full of bologna, and grasping Dave's extended hand and shaking it firmly said, "Doug Forman, rush chairman, damn glad to meet you!" This would forever after be known as the "bologna handshake." I was bent over laughing; trying not to spit up my food at the *Animal House* moment, but Dave was not amused.

"So that's why they call you guys The Fools," he said dryly, looking at the lunch meat clinging to his palm. "I hope your music is better than your sense of humor," he added, walking back to get another beer. Dave smiled at us and finally got to the real reason he'd come back stage.

"So, guys, I hear this Sharona chick is along for the tour. If she looks anything like her picture on the single, she must be fucking jailbait," he said with a leer. "I didn't see her in the other dressing room, is she around anywhere?"

Chris looked at Dave with some amusement and quipped, "That's not Sharona on the cover, she doesn't look anything like that. The woman in that picture is a model."

"No shit," Dave said, disappointed at not being able to connect the wet dream dots.

"Don't get me wrong, Dave, Sharona's still pretty cute; but she's not seventeen, she's about twenty-five, skinny, dark hair with glasses. I wouldn't throw her out of bed, if you know what I mean" Chris said with a laugh and conspiratorial look that tried to relight the lust in Dave's eyes.

Dave looked sadly at Chris, as if not wanting

to ponder the things that Chris wouldn't throw out of bed and said, "Um, alright, I'll see you Fools next time, and remember what I said, change that goddam name!"

With that, he left the room in search of better named bands with younger girlfriends.

"What an asshole," Gino announced, which was exactly what every single one of us down to a man was thinking.

"Mmmph," Doug said in agreement, with a mouthful of bologna and cheese sandwich.

In 1979, The Knack could have played almost anywhere in America and caused a stir, but they seemed to want to play the sell out game. I'm not talking about the alleged "sellout" of letting some huge automotive conglomerate use your song in an ad during the Super Bowl. No, by using the phrase sell out (notice two words, not one) I mean all of the available tickets at a given venue were sold. There is a way of approaching the world of showbiz that never makes you look bad; you only play places you know will completely sell out and The Knack believed fully in that philosophy. Over time, if played correctly, you become a very hot item.

The down side of this approach is mostly financial. If you're smoking hot, why play the five thousand seat capacity theater, when you might sell out the fifteen thousand seat arena? The answer seemed to be that the management people running The Knack seemed to like photos of people standing in line for a ticket more than they liked people actually buying tickets. The long view of an approach like this sees your band, loaded with many more years of hits to come, climbing the rock ladder of success, and waving the middle finger of achievement to all those who doubted you.

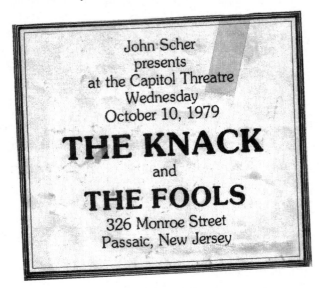

The down side of this approach is that by alienating people in the biz, you better write hit after hit, or you're fucked.

In the five weeks we toured America with them, it always seemed like we should be playing the next biggest place. We of course had no problem with any of it because it wasn't our tour, and any place outside of our New England comfort zone was new and exciting to us. It was also cool to witness a fan "mania" first hand and to see the feeding frenzy that takes place around whatever hot new act is crowned this year's model….mmmm, who's got that new car smell?

Fame can be fleeting however and there would be no more Sharona type hits for The Knack. Their second album *But The Little Girls Understand* didn't do much and whether it would have helped or not, they had no great wealth of radio relationships to draw back upon. In the clear vision of retrospect, it seems that The Knack chose a restrictive, secretive and paranoid path at a time when the whole world of rock was theirs for the taking. Now it's hard to find anyone who even remembers liking them. It's strange that even classic rock stations that specialize in eighties rock tunes rarely play 'My Sharona.'

Throughout this tour, our first honest to God extended rock road experience, we traveled in a tour bus for the first time. It's hard to explain the palpitations I felt when that enormous beast first pulled up to collect us all from a parking lot in Ipswich on that warm summer's day, but even Gino was impressed. Some of the local miners shortened their lunch break at a nearby diner to view the moment, and the town newspaper paper also chronicled the event. It may still be the only time a rock n' roll tour bus ever pulled into Ipswich. It was our John Phillip Souza moment.

I don't care who you are; Bob Dylan, Bruce Springsteen, U2, or any new act coming around today, the first time you ever climb onto a tour bus, you feel like you've made it. Allow me to take you, the uninitiated, through the magic of it all; you walk up the steps, pass the driver's area and enter what can only be called the game room. Lavish couches, pool tables and tastefully appointed chess and backgammon gaming areas await you. Fully stocked bars, refrigerators packed with the best late night choices and a small but efficient kitchen, all overlooked by a state of the art entertainment center, makes this area the hub of any band's day or night time activity.

And speaking of night time, where will all of these highly creative and intensely needy people sleep? Well let's walk down the hall where we'll find private and spacious bedrooms on either side, each with its own bathroom and a windowed view of America whipping by. Finally, at the back of the bus is the function room; a large area, usually reserved for either band rehearsals or the enormous egos of anyone who demands the space as a private area. As the lead singer, I would demand this space more than once.

Okay, I'm just fucking with you; tour buses really aren't all that great. Yes, they have TVs and bathrooms and a small common area just behind the driver, but the sleeping arrangements are horrendous.

On either side of the hall running down the center aisle, there are four to six coffin sized bunks, barely large enough for you and some of your most important things. It really is your only place to get away from everything, but even that won't work if you don't bring earplugs.

Over the years of traveling in these behemoths, I found it important for my own state of mind to verify, at least to myself, that the driver was a sober, straight thinking individual. That way, when the bus lurched or skidded in the middle of the night, I could sigh and go back to some semblance of sleep.

Living this closely, even with people you love, is unnatural. While it might look spectacular, bedecked with some band's logo as it pulls up to a concert hall somewhere in America, more often than not, it contains a small group of men who have been way too close to each other for way too long a time.

After five weeks of watching how not to endear yourselves to the media and trying to sleep on the tour bus, we returned to Ipswich to play a few local gigs and have some meetings with Peter. For a while we'd been trying to decide who should produce our first record and the field was finally narrowing.

As a band, we thought it was important that whoever was hired got our musical take on things, but we were also antsy to start. Peter seemed to think that finding a hot young producer was priority number one. I should explain that last comment, because the meaning of certain words has changed over the years and saying that Peter was looking for a "hot young producer" made him sound gay. He wasn't.

The heat he was looking for in a producer was someone quickly rising up through the ranks that could give us a "sound." That was the supposed gift of producers back then; it was as if all of us young bands were stupid lumps of clay awaiting the Magi's touch to awaken the lost chord within us. What a bunch of crap.

If you'd have heard The Cars when WBCN was playing the cassette tape that the band had produced and given them before they got signed, you would have thought what everyone else thought when they heard it; great band, great song. We'd certainly gotten our own national mileage out of our essentially self-produced (and crappy sounding) cassettes that had wandered around the country.

At this point in time however the music industry had anointed a host of young producer stars who acted as if they were the true magic behind any band's success. Don't understand me wrong, as an Egyptian friend of mine says, I'm not in favor of bands sounding thin, or anything less than ear perfect, but maybe that's where a good engineer comes in. Yes, there were some very talented men, who in some cases, brought out the best in whatever band they were producing. Seriously though, when was the last time you heard a favorite song, from any era, and thought that it sounded too poorly recorded for you to dig the tune?

In the forties and fifties, songs were most often recorded live with only one or two microphones in the room with just an experienced engineer to make that part happen, but it was still all about the song and its captured performance. Do you really think that The Beatles would have wandered away into obscurity without George Martin? Yes, he was the perfect man for the job, and yes it's hard to imagine the Beatles without him...but he wrote no songs; that was left to the three almost Mount Rushmore songwriters in the band.

Sam Phillips is considered to be the first great rock producer, in that he first recorded or signed people like Elvis, Jerry Lee Lewis, Carl Perkins and Roy Orbison. The conventional thinking seems to be that he scoured the bushes and found, and then polished some diamonds. Who knows where rock music would be without Sam Phillips, blah, blah, blah. This type of thinking treats all of these music giants like lost children, as if they were wandering the world without direction or purpose.

The truth is that these people would have found a way to get out that thing that they did, whether there was a Sam Phillips or not. To his credit, he was in the right place, doing the right thing, at the right time. It's all about the songs and the artists; if they're great songs, performed well by great artists, the rest is easy; even if you're Roy Thomas Baker working with Queen, The Cars and Ozzy. Once again, do all of these great bands either disappear, or release musical garbage without Baker? Of course not!

A producer's job is to enhance the product and the best of them do that very well. Okay, I admit I might be overstating my point here, but then again maybe not, seeing as how all these years later, modern recording technology has unlocked the keys to the kingdom and put many of these same producer people out of work. Nowadays a band can buy something about the size of a suitcase, a studio in a box if you will, and experiment with a vast library of sounds. Many successful bands now produce themselves.

When The Knack tour ended, we were introduced to a young Brit producer named Pete Solley who, with his engineer partner Steve Brown, initially seemed like a good fit for us. Pete knew his way around a studio and had played keyboards in some British bands, the most notable being Procol Harum. But this was Procol Harum ten years after the great classic, 'Whiter Shade of Pale,' and by the time Pete joined them for what would be their last album, they'd become a very serious, almost Gothic rock band. It wouldn't be too much of a stretch to say that the brilliant movie *This is Spinal Tap* was based on angst filled, poetry ridden bands like this.

I mention this because Pete never seemed to get what we were doing. My sense is that he probably thought we were some kind of goof. Even if he did get us, he fully agreed with our manager Peter that we needed to be steered away from all forms of silliness. Rock n' roll is serious business dammit, what the hell are you Fools trying to prove? In any event, songs were chosen from the bunch we'd written and on December 7, 1979, Pearl Harbor Day, we began recording our first album Sold Out at Coconut Studios in Florida.

Our manager reminded us more than once heading into the studio that since we were well rehearsed and knew the material, the project should go quickly. We were also told that The Knack had finished their first album in eleven days. The gauntlet had been thrown, the track meet was on. Pete Solley was already down there, having just finished recording a first album for a band from Detroit called The Romantics.

Rich after a long studio session

Before we started recording our stuff, he played us a cut he'd just finished mixing called 'What I Like About You,' that just jumped off the speakers.

I remember thinking it was the best new song I'd heard in a long time. Years later, I read an interview where Pete said he wrote some of that song but wasn't credited. Was this an example of another producer taking credit for the creation of a band's finest work? Who knows, but if he did write half of it, he must wince every time that song is used to sell a car, a hamburger, a soft drink, a feminine hygiene product or a fucking potato peeler. Let's face it, that song might be the all time winner in number of commercials played in.

Pete went on to produce some fine records by Motorhead, Peter Frampton, and far right-wing whack job Ted Nugent, among others so the sting of not getting writing credit may have been tempered by his great success producing records.

For better or worse, Pete never offered to help us write an all-time classic, and our record was finished in eleven days, tying The Knack's recording schedule. Rich would fly back down for a week in January to get involved with Pete and Steve when they did final mixes. There weren't any major changes made to any of the songs, they just sounded better than when we'd recorded the old cassettes on our own.

With our first album in the can, the band arrived back in Ipswich a few days before Christmas and we had our first real stretch of time off in almost three years. A lot had happened, a lot more would happen, but this downtime was needed for a mental and physical health break. Perhaps an illustration of my state of mind at the time is in order: I was awoken in the middle of the night, a few days after Christmas by Ginny, who was poking me awake and saying, "What weird sponge? What were you talking about?"

"Huh?" I said, still half asleep.

"What about the weird sponge?" she repeated.

"I don't know what you're talking about," I said starting to get irritated, "maybe I was talking in my sleep."

"No," she replied, as if she knew I must be joking, "you just sat up in bed, and in a very clear voice said 'behold the weird sponge,' then you laid back down."

I still don't know what the hell was going on in my sleeping brain that night, but it sounds like it was important and I always wanted to use that phrase somewhere, sometime. I just did.

CHAPTER NINE

Pay No Attention to the Man Behind the Curtain!

Steppenwolf, Rick Derringer, Southside Johnny, The Ramones, The J. Geils Band, The Doobie Brothers, The Cars, Rush, Van Halen, The Plasmatics, The Motels, The Knack, Blondie, The Bangles, Kansas, Toto, Billy Squier, Los Lobos, Motorhead, Joan Jett, Katrina and the Waves, til tuesday, The Pointer Sisters, Eric Burden, Alvin Lee, Jefferson Starship,

Peter Gabriel, Cheap Trick, Eric Carmen, Journey, Kate Bush, Donovan, David Johansen, The Joe Perry Project, Roger McGuinn, A Flock of Seagulls, Lenny Clarke, Steve Sweeney

The band with comedian Lenny Clarke   and Sam Kinison.

I know there are many more, but these are just some of the bands or comedians we've either toured with, backed up for a night or two or appeared with on a Euro-TV show.

Just like no one starts out playing baseball thinking, "I wish I could play in the minor leagues," I doubt if anyone ever started touring America thinking,

"I wish I could be in a backup band." Backup bands are people who are striving to make their own mark in the world, not grease the nightly party wheels for whatever headliner is closing the show. Most, if not all openers, wish they were the main act.

I say most because we once opened for Wendy O. Williams and The Plasmatics and I couldn't wait to get offstage and get out of there. But I didn't; I stayed and watched the Viking-esque insanity that was their show, complete with the enormous burning wooden symbols, the pounding metal music and the ritual chainsaw destruction of a TV set, conducted by the gorgeous bikini clad Wendy, that crowned the end of the performance. It was crazy and yet wonderful: it had the visual feel of a Wagnerian opera, combined with the stance of punk/metal rock. The reason I wanted to get out of there had nothing to do with The Plasmatics, it was because of the audience.

If any band ever had a porno crowd appeal, it was The Plasmatics. This was the world before internet porn, and I guess you had to get it where you could, so while the audience had a high percentage of rock fans, it also had a high percentage of older, single, creepy men. That made it an extremely tough crowd to play for because there was no galvanizing factor. There were the "I like her music" people, and the "I like her music and the fact that she's almost naked" people, and then finally there were the "is it ok if I jerk off into my popcorn box?" people.

Wendy would wear as little or less than the law allowed and years before Madonna and others, she was toying with the performance standards of the rock world.

Backstage however, Wendy was a genuine sweetheart, autographing pictures for any and all, and seeming like the happy, but twisted girl next door. She thought we were funny, and she seemed to like that she wasn't the only one out there playing a character onstage. The difference was, if I stripped down to my underwear, or got naked onstage, or put on a cowboy hat, it was just a goofy, stupid thing to get the place amped up and probably most importantly, I never got arrested. But if she came out with nothing but whipped cream covering her nipples and her genitals (why didn't I think of that?) it was somehow pornographic.

Once again, you can fuck with people's government, you can fuck with people's laws, you can even fuck with whether people can say the word fuck, but don't mess with their entertainment. Wendy got arrested more than once for her performance art, and it may have just come down to her reputation coupled with the local pressure any town official felt when her sideshow was coming to town. I could almost hear them thinking.

Police Chief: "Just want to let you know that Wendy O's band is coming to town. There could be some problems."

Mayor: "What kinda problems, Chief?"

Police Chief: "Well, she strips down to almost nothing and cuts up a TV with a real chainsaw."

Mayor: "A TV, no shit, what's she look like?"

Police Chief: "She's a freakin' babe."

Mayor: "Okay, arrest her...but do it after the show and get me some tickets."

Many bands we played with were in the midst of taking over the musical world. In 1980, we had the great pleasure of playing three nights with The J. Geils Band in Detroit when their Love Stinks album came out. Though they were finally becoming huge across America, Wolf and the Geils Band already owned Detroit down to the last hubcap; a working class band being deified by a working class town. Since I'd seen them from their beginnings in my little coal mining town, and we'd played with them at the Cape Cod Coliseum, I was totally on board for the coronation.

It was a great rock crowd to play for but I felt somewhat frustrated after our thirty minute set. While we got a good response from those in the house who were actually playing attention, there were still people just finding their seats for the main act and I thought we could have done better.

Later that night, at an after-hours party, I mentioned my frustration to Geils' drummer Stephen

Jo Bladd and he said something like this: "Don't feel bad, we backed up The Who and there were people in the audience with their backs to us as if we weren't worthy of being in the same building with the band they had come to see."

The Love Stinks album seemed to finally put the great Geils band into the national argument as to who was the best American rock band.

It wasn't always about flash and street style though; once we were doing a rock TV show in Germany called *RockPop* with Journey, and

though they'd already had some major hits in the seventies, they had just finished their eighth album, *Escape*, and they knew they had a monster on deck. I remember talking to lead singer Steve Perry in a stairwell in between taping songs for the show, and he was almost reverent about what they'd just recorded. I remember him saying, "I know we have it."

And they did, at last count, *Escape*, with hits like, 'Don't Stop Believin' and 'Open Arms' has sold over nine million records; not to mention the dozens of commercials, movies and televisions shows those songs have appeared in.

Ok, kids, now it's time for a quick pop quiz: name the band that ranks fourth all-time (behind The Beatles, The Stones, and Aerosmith) in consecutive number of Gold or Platinum albums. There are so many contenders that leap to mind but most of them don't make the cut because these miss out on the two most vital ingredients, longevity and continued success. Almost no one comes up with the correct answer, unless this hint is thrown in; they're from Canada. Still thinking…well time's up and the answer of course is Rush.

We opened for Rush a few times, and they are numero uno on our all time list of "Treating The Opening Band Like Human Beings." (If you were curious, Van Halen would be dead last, but that story my friends deserves an entire chapter of its own). Once Rush actually kept an arena's doors from opening until after we (the fucking opening guys!) got our sound check and wonder of wonders, when we backed them at the Providence Civic Center in Rhode Island; they even put a little extra dough in our pay.

I wish I could take it personally and say that we were one of their favorite bands; singer Geddy Lee did seem to enjoy our irreverence and drummer Neil Peart seemed to think we were a hard working and entertaining band. In hindsight, it probably had as much to do with their Libertarian political views as anything else.

I would be surprised to learn that they ever treated an opening act like crap, and as far as the extra money at the Civic Center gig was concerned, they knew we'd put a few fans of our own in the house that night. The latter wouldn't have mattered to almost any other headlining band on the planet, but refreshingly, Rush is a band that lives its politics, and I don't think they'd do it any other way. That could be one reason why forty years into it, they're still going strong and packing arenas all over the world.

One thing I remember about Geddy; he had a good sense of humor. Although I didn't use it when we played with them, I had a goalie hockey stick fitted with a guitar strap that I was messing around with during a sound check. I saw Geddy watching and smiling offstage, so I walked over thinking maybe we'd talk a little hockey, me being a Bruins' fan and him being, well...a Canadian. But to my surprise, after seeing me wearing a Red Sox cap, he wanted to talk a little baseball. I can talk baseball with anyone at any time, and I think maybe Geddy can too, because he knew his stuff. I seem to recall him looking forward to a Fenway Park visit, and he had sympathy with my then, still star crossed Red Sox team.

Sometimes you see things backstage that maybe you aren't supposed to see. I'm not talking about drug use, or screaming rock star fits, or even the odd band girlfriend going *Spinal Tap* on some poor band member or roadie.

Yes, I've seen lots of that shit, and even fallen victim to much of the same, and I know that those salacious details probably appeal to some of you readers. But let's now come to an agreement; just accept that a band with none of the previously listed problems or issues is almost unheard of. So if you want to ask me if this guy or that guy did drugs, or banged somebody's girlfriend, or hit a bucket of golf balls off of a parking lot roof in LA, or climbed an eighty foot water tower, smoked a joint and then got too scared to come down, let's just say yes to all of it, and just maybe we'll get back to those subjects later.

One thing I'm going to tell you may not impress or even surprise you, but it impressed the hell out of me and the other guys in the band. We were opening for the band Toto (you'll remember them from MTV staples such as 'Africa,' and 'Rosanna') somewhere in the Midwest for a couple of nights when Chris and I, walking backstage, noticed a guy getting set up behind the curtain, looking like he was going to sing something. He was dressed in typical rock star attire and a roadie was setting him up with headphones and a microphone.

We were interested, but we didn't say anything to the backstage dude. We kept our distance and watched, wondering what part he might have in the show. Toto began their show, and a few songs into their set, our guy stood up and, during one of the more challenging vocal parts, he sang a high harmony to what was going on out front, then he sat down in his chair and waited. Chris and I were floored, and this unassuming guy soon became our hero as he sang his occasional vocals backstage, behind a curtain, unnoticed and un-applauded.

The next night, Chris and I brought some beer, and set up chairs about twenty feet away from the mystery singer with the great voice and when he would belt out the stuff that the onstage guys couldn't do, we clapped for him. Strangely enough, he bowed towards us, sat down and awaited his next moment.

The best thing about this story is of course that the band's name was Toto, which I always assumed was a reference to The Wizard of Oz. One of the most iconic scenes from that film was Dorothy, her friends and her little dog Toto being told by the wizard to "pay no attention to the man behind the curtain." I remember Toto as a band that played their stuff really well, but I always wondered if the guys in Toto ever got the irony of the situation with the man behind their very own curtain.

Not long after the Toto tour, I mentioned this story to Boston's Brad Delp, and he had an interesting take on the guy backstage. "I wish I had one," he said, and even though I never heard Brad sing a bad note, I understood what he meant.

The Great Voices are under enormous pressure

to do that thing that they do, day in and out, in sickness and in health, for as long as they all shall live. They're like hot young movie starlets that have to compete with the younger, on screen versions of themselves when they get older. The difference is that plastic surgery and really good makeup can disguise the age of a movie star, at least for a while, but nothing can disguise a voice that can no longer hit the notes. I completely understand why Robert Plant doesn't want to sing Led Zeppelin songs now that he's an older guy; he can't. How can he compete with himself at twenty one?

I saw the man known as "The Voice," Roy freakin' Orbison mess up the climbing vocal during 'In Dreams' and stop the band in front of a few thousand people. The house got quiet. But then the grand master of all things vocal said nothing, sipped

a bottle of water, and the band and he restarted and brought the song to a resounding completion that left the audience standing, cheering and delirious. I saw Roy many times, and maybe his only secret was, amazingly, that he smoked a lot of cigarettes.

I once had the chance

to meet Roy; we'd reverently covered his classic 'Running Scared' on our second album *Heavy Mental*, and he was playing at the Hampton Beach Casino in New Hampshire a week after us. I got my front row tickets and the Casino management figured that it was a lock that I would want to meet him.

They led me backstage and opened the door to his dressing room and I saw it was filled with well wishers, band mates and the usual hangers on, and there in the corner dealing with it all was Roy. I wore thick glasses in high school, and always covered one Roy tune or another in any band I was in. For this reason my nickname for a while was *Orba*, and some longtime friends still call me that on occasion, but that wasn't my real connection with him. The connection was the same one he had with millions of other fans; his ability to absolutely nail the intensity of the man/women thing, and somehow give you, the heartbroken, a temporary cathartic feeling in the course of a two and a half minute song. It was truly a magic act, but Roy was no flim-flam guy, he was the real deal.

I have no regrets over the following: rather than be another guy saying to him, "You are the best fucking singer that ever lived, no really, I mean it...do you understand how important you are to me, and can you please sign this, and how about a picture of me and you,"...rather than be that guy, I turned around and left. I like to think that leaving was my tiny gift to Roy.

Sometimes, it's better to think of your heroes doing the songs you love, than it is to think of them dealing with another person like you, or worse yet, you find out that your hero is not the person you perceive him to be. In that respect however, I've never read a bad word about Roy.

Many performers, when they're onstage, seem like that best friend we are destined to have, but never did. They light some lamp in us; they speak for what we can't put into words, they walk effortlessly from spotlight to stage edge, and they dance and move and sing like we want to, if only we weren't locked into our minds and bodies. They exist in a dream we have about how the best of us can be, and at least for the length of a show, or even a song, the dream is real.

CHAPTER TEN
Far Flung Fools

"Let us swear while we may, for in heaven it will not be allowed."
                                    Mark Twain

Peter was his usual impeccably dressed self; tan suit with matching loafers, and white shirt opened at the collar. He was every bit the suave and competent rock manager, and tonight was another example of Peter at the top of his game. He'd organized a national forty station FM broadcast from a club on Long Island for tonight, April 1, 1980, to celebrate the release of our first album Sold Out which would kick off our first headlining national tour.

Doing a live radio show was a fairly common occurrence back in the seventies and eighties before MTV was the primary way for a band to build popularity. Many bands broke big first regionally and then nationally by the way of a live broadcast.

U2 had done it with their legendary 1981 show that WBCN in Boston sent out over the airwaves. That station, which supported us so well, is often credited with introducing U2, a then unknown Irish band, to America. And here we were, a year earlier, getting ready to blast our stuff out over the airwaves.

The club, a cool joint called My Father's Place

was packed, and we were about an hour from show time.

"Okay guys, this is important, are we all feeling good?" Peter asked, nervously pacing and asking the room in general but looking at Doug and me in particular. It wasn't just because the two of us ran the onstage show; Peter had other concerns in mind.

In Doug's case he was just coming off of the flu, but in my case, I'd once gone swimming in a hotel pool the night before one of our most important record company auditions and lost my contact lenses. Peter had tried to get the hotel to drain the pool and check the filter for my lenses. They declined. As luck would have it, I had one spare contact with me, so I was able to go onstage only half blind and the audition was saved.

But numerous foolish things like my lost contacts were beginning to leave a mark on Peter and he was taking no chances. He was like a school teacher taking a special needs class on an extended field trip, it might be fun and even rewarding on some level, but there weren't going to be many relaxing moments.

"The other thing is," Peter continued, "you guys can't swear. Remember this isn't WBCN in Boston, the rest of the country is pretty strict about that kind of stuff."

"What can't we say?" Chris asked innocently, trying to get Peter to swear. Peter never swore.

But our manager wasn't playing along. "Do you understand what a swear is?" he asked Chris.

"He means you can't say fuck," Gino said, smiling from across the room, his bald head perfectly groomed and shining. Gino had placed his large body, with arms folded, against the closed door to our dressing room. He did that sort of thing without ever thinking about it. He would have made a perfect palace guard.

"Not just that word," said Peter, "any swears of any kind. This has to be a clean show." He looked around the room to see if we were getting it.

"What about hell," I asked thoughtfully. "Everybody says hell, it's not really a swear, is it?"

"I think hell is okay," Peter answered with some condescension, but with no hint of irony in his voice.

"What about shit?" Doug asked, looking up from tuning his bass. "Everybody says shit. Can we say shit?"

"Why would you need to?" Peter asked, becoming slowly exasperated and honestly puzzled by where the conversation was going.

"Why would you need to?" he repeated, as if saying it twice made even the question all the more valid.

"Shit happens," Rich replied in explanation. I grunted my approval at his perfect placement of a stupid phrase. As I noted before, Rich has always had the ability to sum up a situation in a very few words. The best part was he also knew it was a stupid phrase.

"You don't need to say shit," I said to the room in general with my pointing finger in the air, "if you substitute words like poopoo and caca." I paused for effect and added solemnly in Peter's direction, "and let's not forget doody."

"Doody is good," Chris said begrudgingly with his hand on his chin, as if he were the final say in all things of this nature.

Peter was nodding his head slowly, and looking at us like a guy who may have picked the wrong horse in a race. In our defense, this kind of nonsense made us relax, but it generally sent Peter into extended pacing, and the need for someone, anyone in the band to acknowledge whatever important point he was trying to make.

But it was Stacey who finally brought the pullets

home to rest when he asked. "So what happens when we play 'Psycho Chicken?'" The room got quiet.

"Oh shit," Gino whispered quietly to himself at the door, forgetting the new rules. Stacey had raised a good question; because the song that had put us on the map, 'Psycho Chicken,' contained the winsome shouted phrase "What the Fuck!" It didn't just happen once in the song, it was a recurring motif.

To the end of making us a more viable national product, and not a novelty act, Peter, and EMI had convinced us that the song should not even be included on our debut album. Instead it was added as an insert, a 45 single of the song literally included in only the first forty thousand or so albums. Peter wanted that song and any memory of it put in our rear view mirror for the sake of the Big Picture. To those of you who have that single tucked away in your attic, it might make you a little cash on eBay.

"Just put it in the encore," Peter said after a few seconds of thought. "The live broadcast will be over by then."

This made sense to all of us, but Chris couldn't help himself from asking Peter one more question.

"I don't know if all of us are clear on the swearing thing….we can say hell, but we can't say shit. Is that right?"

We all looked at Peter as if Chris had raised a good point. Peter sighed, looked at all of us, took a deep breath and said:

"You fucking assholes, you can't say shit, you can't say cocksucker, you can't say pussy, you can't say motherfucker..." he was starting to shout, he had our full attention and some of us were clapping and yelling 'yea' after each phrase. "...you can't say prick, you can't say shitlapper, you can't say bumfucker, you can't say tits, and you most definitely cannot fucking say what the fuck!"

With that, Peter spun on his heel and headed for the door, which Gino, with a nod and a slight flourish opened for him.

"Geezus," Doug said, "shitlapper?"

***

"Ladies and gentlemen, please welcome EMI recording artists, The Fools!"

We jumped into 'Spent the Rent' and with good energy and open eyes we blasted our tunes out across America's radio stations. My memory of the night is that we played well and stood tall. You can judge that for yourself if you can ever find an album called, The *First Annual Official Unofficial April Fools Day Live Bootleg.*

EMI decided to take the night's recordings, and make a limited release of a few thousand albums, which were then to be handed out to such "friendlies" as DJ's, record reps, and promo people. But now, with eBay, procuring almost anything is possible, so you can probably find it. And you can probably still get rare signed copies of Nate and Ida's wedding, filmed at the Masonic Temple in Asspork, Wisconsin without too much trouble. By the way, I saw that wedding and it's a steal at $19.95.

Fools Day Live Bootleg

There is however something that you won't hear on the live recording of that night and it's really a shame that it went undocumented. We'd been told by whoever was overseeing the recording, that at the halfway mark of the sixty minute broadcast, we'd go to commercials for ninety seconds, and at that point, we would only be heard by the club's live audience. This created moment in a live show seemed, to us, ripe for tomfoolery.

In grade school, when the teacher said, "the next one that laughs is in trouble," it was always me. It wasn't that I was a brazen little bastard, I was actually quite shy. It was more my response to the unbearable and exquisite possibility of filling that quiet moment that got me in trouble.

This situation was a little bit different; in the middle of a show we were going to stop for a sort of station break so that stations around the country could give their call letters and go to their local commercials. I think we were expected to either stand there, or make small talk with the audience. We did neither. Instead it went something like this:

"Hey, we have to take a little break now so that all the stations around the country can give their call letters. So this is our chance to really talk to you people. I think that so far we're giving you everything we have. Doug, have we left anything out of this show?"

"Funny you should ask Mike, but yes we have. So far we haven't done any swearing at all."

"No swearing! What the fuck?"

The audience was laughing, and even Peter on the side of the stage seemed to be into the joke.

"Is there any way we can fix that, you fucking asshole?" I asked Doug.

"Yes Mike, you cocksucker," Doug said, "we can swear for the next minute until the stations come back from commercials."

And we did, with much repetition, because after

about twenty seconds, you start throwing in weird stuff like shitlapper. There was much laughter and a feeling like we'd made a special, grade school connection with the audience. Then suddenly the news came in the form of a note quickly handed to me by an unusually stern looking Gino which read: NOT ALL STATIONS WENT TO COMMERCIAL, STOP SWEARING!

My chin dropped, and I elbowed Doug, who was running on about blowjobs or something, when I handed him the note. I could see his face flush like mine must have. We looked over to the side of the stage and were told that we were back live in about ten seconds. "Back live," I said, "when were we ever dead?"

The second half of the show was quite a bit more subdued, partly because of the notes that continued to come from the side of the stage. Like messages announcing damages from an interstellar nuclear war, I read things like: WE'VE JUST LOST SEATTLE and ALBUQUERQUE GONE, and finally ALL OF TEXAS GONE. It turned out that our little grade school connection with a couple of hundred people had cost us a portion of our national audience.

It's funny how times change; back then news of this nature wouldn't have been more than a blurb in any city's Arts and Entertainment section, with us being the dumb asses. Now, if it happened, it would not only be deliberate, but that band's promo machine would squeeze the last outrageous drop out of it, and the band would be christened the new bad boys of rock.

At the end of the night, what should have been a celebration, not only of our grand introduction to the nation, but of Peter's great organizational skills, was pretty low key. There was a bit of a bunker mentality as we looked over the night's victories and defeats, but Peter was surprisingly upbeat. After all, America was awaiting us, in the form of seventeen straight one-nighters which would take us from Long Island into the Midwest. Our next day off would be in Wisconsin, and it came just in time.

CHAPTER ELEVEN

Really Nailing it on the Road

Being in a touring band, we've seen some amazing things over the years that you just wouldn't see if you're not in a band or traveling carnival. It's not just the idea of going town to town across the lower forty-eight because countless tourists have done that; it's more the view you get when you're playing in smaller venues. I could make the case that even arena bands that have traveled the globe for years, are missing the real music experience of playing in all the little fascinating joints of the world.

It can be an antiseptic view of humanity to be separated from the adoring crowds each night by the setup and stance of the arena style show. It's another whole thing to be face to face each night, playing to hundreds of people instead of thousands. In more intimate settings, you get a feeling that the show's success or failure has a communal factor to it; both the audience and the band are combining to make it all happen. The early Blues Masters, as well as the early Kings of Country and Rockabilly music wrote the book on this kind of thing in the fifties.

Long before there was even a concept of getting twenty-thousand people to go to a music show, there were great bands, from Muddy Waters to Hank Williams, from Jerry Lee Lewis to BB King that were touring throughout America and playing in its honky-tonks and juke joints. And when the band was kickin' it, and the audience was jumpin', it must have felt like the circus had come to town.

Some of the places are eccentric and well known to everyone within a hundred miles. We played in a club that had an honest to God pet Cheetah that spent most of its time lounging on the second story roof adjacent to the band dressing room.

Another place had an enormous boa constrictor living in a glass cage built into the dance floor. We've played in places that had strippers on in between sets, and other places where bikers drove their bikes into the clubs during our show.

On day sixteen of our opening seventeen straight one-nighters, we were somewhere in or near Wisconsin, playing a small but packed club and I'd just grabbed a chair to stand on. The band was grinding out the final chord of the last song and, since the stage wasn't very high, I wanted to get up a little higher before I jumped up and came down to land on the stage ending the show with a flair. I leaped up, thinking I was a good bit under the low ceiling.

I wasn't, and this next part is not for the squeamish; at the height of my jump, my head struck a nail sticking down from the ceiling. I felt something hit my head, but such is the energy of a good show, that I ignored it and headed for the dressing room while the audience yelled for an encore.

One of my many leaps

Rich was behind me and in a very serious tone asked, "Are you ok? What happened to you?" All the while he was firmly leading me to a chair and calling for Gino. On that night I was wearing a white sports coat over a black shirt and checkered pants (hey, we were new wave) and the back of my white coat was covered in blood. I still wasn't feeling any pain, and I convinced everyone that the bleeding was mostly stopped, so I took off my jacket, and headed back to the stage.

We did one quick tune, I came off stage, Gino wrapped my head in a towel, and took me to the nearest hospital. The doctor wanted to shave out an area around the wound, but I talked him out of it. He said the cut was more like a gouge, and there wasn't any skin to pull together for stitching, so he gave me a tetanus shot and some disinfectant, and in short order I was back on the tour bus in time for a beer and a game of Scrabble. The joke the next day had to do with my ability to jump in the air and stay up for a while, my 'hang time' being aided by the nail attaching me to the ceiling.

The next night we were playing a club in Madison, our last gig before a few days off. I was cranky and I had a headache, but the show started to cheer me up. We placed 'Psycho Chicken' about halfway into the set. We weren't playing it all the time, mostly to appease Peter, but in some college towns like Madison, we knew it had gotten airplay. When the song started, I jumped down into the crowd of three hundred or so and tried to get them to join in the singing of the "What the Fuck!" part.

All of a sudden, the microphone was being grabbed out of my hand by some local loony that was apparently upset by our parody of a Talking Heads' song. Since I refused to give up the mic, we both ended up rolling on the floor in the midst of the crowd.

Though they'd lost sight of me, the band kept playing. Within seconds of the scrum starting, I felt myself lifted up and away by Gino, who calmly and efficiently turned around and walked back to the stage clearing a path as he went. His manner of clearing a path was simple; he looked directly at those in front of him and walked straight at them. They moved.

Gino was not one to fuck with. We got to the stage, he placed me on it, and I finished the song, which hadn't stopped. The rest of the night went smoothly, and so ended the first leg of the First Fools World Tour.

CHAPTER TWELVE

Bigfoot Stole My Wife

"...the reality of the phenomenon of Bigfoot cannot be denied."
Loren Coleman, Cryptozoologist

There's something about the Great Plains of America that can truly mess with your mind; and not just if you're in a whacked out, drug addled, beer swilling rock band. This part of the country is so flat, grassy, and featureless, that I'm guessing that even the billion odd storied buffalo of times past, after gorging themselves silly on the abounding high grade vegetation, must have had trouble describing their next destination to their buffalo friends.

Buffalo no. 1: "Ok, there's a five foot tall rock about three hundred miles west of here. If there's no stampede, and the Indians don't kill us, I'll meet you there in two weeks."

Buffalo no. 2: "The rock is good, but if we get separated, I'll meet you at the tree."

Buffalo no. 1: "You're not talking the bush right, 'cause I hate the bush; there's too many flies."

Buffalo no. 2: "No, I'm talking the tree, a hundred miles south of the rock."

Buffalo no. 1 "Ok, the tree is good, but don't tell anyone else; if there's a half a million other buffalo there, we'll never get near it."

Nowadays the rock, the bush, and the tree have different names; like Tulsa, Topeka, and Omaha.

They continue to be every bit as welcome to the four wheeled traveler as they were to the four hoofed; especially after blasting along straight lined highways through corn and wheat fields for hours on end.

We in the band, when not rehashing the previous night's gig, or lying about some past event, mostly read books, played Scrabble, backgammon, poker, and chess, and tried not to look out the window. A strange but very comfortable schizophrenia starts to set in after a few weeks on the road; the days on the bus are limbo-like; boring and restful, and the nights on stage are fully alive and exhilarating.

Our bus driver for this leg of our tour was a somber fellow, who kept totally apart from us, and though he seemed to be every bit the competent driver, he sometimes got a faraway crazy look in his eye when we asked him about touring with other bands. After much prying, we learned that he'd been driving tour busses for years, and had driven some of the greats; The Allman Brothers, Chuck Berry, and Creedence. He didn't seem to be much of a music fan, so he didn't have any good stories about seeing this or that memorable show. He only knew people by how they acted on the tour bus, and most of the bands he'd driven were pretty tame once they got off stage.

The exception seemed to be David Bowie. He almost shivered when he mentioned his name.

"They were crazy," he said, when talking of Bowie's band with the kind of awe and respect you would save for a serial killer, but he would say no more.

We always wondered at the level of depravity it took to make a bus driver tremble. This intrigued us because, over the last two months, this man had seen us do all sorts of odd things; from hanging our bare asses out the window at a belligerent trucker, to sneaking onto the short wave radio and giving bogus traffic reports ("you'll want to stay out of the left lane to avoid a pair of mating moose"), to cooking a shoe in the microwave, and he never blinked. Over the years, this kind of behavior cost us a driver or two; one day we'd look up and there'd be a new guy behind the wheel with no explanation except, "he went home."

Sometimes to pass the time we watched movies, and often enough, just like your oddly focused preschooler, we would watch the same movies over and over again and take pride in learning the dialogue.

The favorite flick on this tour was the great Paul Newman hockey film Slap Shot. We all knew it by heart and, with little or no prompting, we would launch into our favorite scenes, any time, any place.

"I'm talking old time hockey, like Eddie Shore,"

Chris would mutter under his breath while reading the breakfast menu at IHOP.

"Piss on Eddie Shore," I would whisper in answer, wondering if I should get the Grand Slam, or the Belgian waffles.

There were other methods of dealing with the daytime's boredom; sometimes I would retire to my tiny coffin-like sleeping area and write an inspirational "state of the union" speech to keep up band morale. The speech would always borrow heavily from history, fiction, and current band events. Once it was written, I would stand up at the front of the bus next to the driver, and with much throat clearing and paper shuffling, I would bring the assembled group to attention. The typical speech went something like this:

"Dearly beloved we are gathered here today because, four score and seven days ago, we set forth with the intent to spread our foolish words upon this continent. So far the spreading has been good, and we may now count many new converts in such exotic places as Cleveland, Detroit, and Chicago (shouts of hear! hear! filled the bus). And yes, there have been some naysayers; like that friggin' Nazi music reviewer in Wisconsin who said, 'The Fools can't sing, play, or write good songs' [boos and hoots filled the bus]. I know there are some among you, perhaps even me, who want to hunt that bastard down and give him a taste of old time hockey! Get out there on the ice and let 'em know you're there! Get that fuckin' stick in his side; get that lumber in his teeth! Let 'em know you're there! [cheers and table pounding result from this passage straight out of *Slap Shot*] But are we not above such petty things?"

"Yes, we are not," Rich replied ambiguously. The bus driver seemed to be getting nervous.

"Some have even wondered," I continued, "if we were no longer doing God's work of bringing our words to the heathens. For those who still doubt, I will now read to you from the Good Book." I held up a book entitled *1,001 Party Cocktails*. Doug was now eating stale popcorn and throwing pieces of it at me, so I ducked and shifted as I continued.

"How about this passage from Isosceles 28-41, '…and the Lord said who shall smite the people? I need that they shall be smitten. And yea I say unto you that it shall be a fool who shall smiteth them.'"

"Amen," Stacey said. Doug threw popcorn at Stacey as Gino watched with amusement.

"Or how about this line from Follicles Chapter 13, 'It was a fool that I sent among them that he may maketh them laugh, and then poundeth them with a rock.' [more hoots and yells of AMEN!] Friends, it's clear what our mission is, and since we're not playing tonight, let us stop at the next purveyor of potent potables and acquire some thirst quenching quaffs!"

"Huh?" Chris asked.

"Let's buy some beer," Rich explained to noises of approval. Doug threw popcorn at Rich. Chris threw popcorn at Doug. Nobody threw popcorn at Gino.

My speech was now annoying even me. It was time to wrap it up.

"Finally my friends, it troubles me to bring up the next subject, but I would be remiss if I did not. It's come to my attention that someone may have smuggled some cocaine onto the bus."

Gasps of mock horror follow this comment.

"It's not my intention to tell you how to live, or to preach to you on the evils of drugs, let's just say that whoever you are, if you leave the packet of cocaine on the pillow of my bunk, I will dispose of it...no questions asked."

Now everybody was throwing popcorn, and the mood was firmly set for a day of drinking, watching movies, and playing games.

In this manner, we made our way through the Midwest and traveled northwest into Montana. They call Montana "Big Sky Country" and that's probably because your eyes don't seem able to take in the whole picture. The scenery was intense; long, hilly, grassy fields leading to enormous plateaus; and the whole picture dwarfed by the not too distant mountains. The landscape is so wide and huge, it makes you feel that giants must have once walked the earth, and if they did, they were at home in Montana.

After playing a gig in Helena, the following day we headed north towards Canada. Our plan was to cross the border, then go west, and re-enter the US through the state of Washington.

On the trip through northern Montana, you're hugged right up next to the Rocky Mountains, and the country gets pretty wild looking. There are some tiny towns tucked into the foothills, but they're mostly places you could successfully hide someone in the Witness Protection Program.

Let's remember that Helena, the state capitol, barely tops a population of 25,000 people during the height of tourist season (for two weeks in August they have the Take off Your Winter Coat Festival). The towns have names like Buffalo Flap, Broken Wagon, and Bull Urine, and they couldn't have seemed any more exotic to a bunch of kids from an East Coast coal mining town.

As we drove through the grand expanse of countryside, I suddenly remembered reading that Montana has known its share of Bigfoot sightings. The subject has always fascinated me, and since I was a kid, I've read extensively about it. Rich and Stacey are also interested in the field of crypto-zoology, as the study of supposed "hidden animals" is called, so we began talking about it, and the morning passed quickly. Around noon, we radioed to the camper following us that we were going to stop at the next place we saw and get something to eat. The camper contained our soundman Walter, our lighting tech Fritz, and a roadie we all called, interestingly enough, Sasquatch. I don't remember who gave him the nickname, but since he was tall, barrel chested, and hairy, the name stuck.

We finally found a truck stop and all of us, band, Gino, and roadies, went inside and put a couple of tables together to form a big one. We ordered food and the conversation went back to Bigfoot. Rich mentioned that some form of large hairy biped was known by different names all over the world.

"In China they call him *Omah*, in Australia they call him Yowie, and here," he said looking at Sasquatch," they call him you."

Sasquatch giggled and smirked. "You guys believe that shit?"

"There might be something to it," I added, "people as diverse as Marco Polo and Meriwether Clark, of the Lewis and Clark expedition, mention hairy wild men in their journals."

Gino looked meaningfully at Sasquatch and said, "Hairy wild men...these are your people." He had a dry sense of humor.

"I can't believe you guys buy that shit," said Sasquatch, looking sadly at us.

The food came, brought by a hardy, but pleasant

looking, middle aged woman. She was still bringing food to the table when I said, "Sasquatch, pass me the butter."

"That your name, Sasquatch?" She eyed him suspiciously. He hunched down a little in his chair.

"It's our nickname for him," I said, "and I was just telling him that Montana's had some Bigfoot sightings."

The once pleasant woman looked sternly at me and said, "Are you making fun of me?"

"No," I said, surprised by the turn the conversation had taken. "Some of us at this table think they're real, and we were just laughing because our friend, whose nickname is Sasquatch, doesn't believe in them."

She seemed to soften up a little and said, "I can tell you boys ain't from around here, so if you want to hear about Bigfoot, you go ask my husband Bill at the front desk."

As she left Sasquatch turned to me and said, "I don't know how, but you fucking put her up to that, I know you did."

I told him I was good, but not that good, and after we ate, he, Chris and I went to find her husband.

Bill was a big, burly man with a plaid work shirt, and the calm, but serious demeanor of one who would not suffer us Fools gladly. I told him what his wife had said, and he eyed us carefully before telling us this story:

"You boys passed the ranger station about five miles back. Three days ago, my eighteen year old daughter had just passed that on her way to town at about ten o'clock in the morning. She was just making the turn that starts you up that long hill, when something about seven feet tall and walking on two legs crossed the road about fifty yards ahead of her. She said it was covered in long grey hair from head to toe. She slowed down to a stop and watched it walk into the bushes. She then turned the car around and drove back to the ranger station and reported what she saw. Before she even finished her story, the two rangers there jumped into their jeep and peeled off in the direction she'd come from. I'm thinking it's not the first time someone reported something like this."

I looked at Sasquatch, his mouth was open and he was hanging on every word, just like Chris and I. "Geezus," he said quietly.

Bill looked at us with a challenge in his eye, just in case we were going to laugh at his story, and then said flatly, "I don't know what she saw, but my daughter's not a liar."

We stood there in silence for a moment. But then the rest of the band and crew showed up and soon we were out the door and back on our way towards Canada.

The Canadian border was only a few hours away, and by nightfall we were on the other side. It was Gino's job to periodically check in with Peter, and after the phone call, he came back toward the bus with a definite jump in his stride.

The news wasn't always good from New York, although to Peter's credit; he tried to be upbeat about most things. The last bit of news we'd had was that our single, 'It's a Night for Beautiful Girls' was stalled at forty-one on the *Billboard* charts, keeping it just outside of the magic Top Forty. Peter seemed to think that some of the local reps, and the company in general were dropping the ball. So as we watched Gino's large, bald, frame come up to the door of the bus, it was not without some trepidation. But Gino was smiling. The door opened and he announced "we're going to Japan!"

It turned out that against all odds; odds that included the Japanese liking a song that was not released in their country, odds that included them finding a way to get it played on their rock stations even though the single was hard to find, and odds that included the friggin' language barrier...against all these odds,... 'Psycho Chicken,' which roughly translated to *Kichigai Niwatori* in the native language was a big hit in Japan. EMI had arranged for us to fly to Tokyo and play a half-dozen shows as soon as our tour ended in LA. We hit the road again and celebrated long into the night.

One other thing of note happened that day; at around three in the morning, Fritz called from the camper to say that Sasquatch had pulled down all the window curtains, turned all the lights on and seemed to be chain smoking and acting very tense.

"I think he wants to sleep on the bus with you guys; the Bigfoot stuff freaked him out" the bemused Fritz reported. I told Gino what was up and asked him what we should do. He took the phone from me and walked a ways down the bus. When he came back I asked him what had happened. He said he'd had a talk with Sasquatch.

"What did you say," I asked.

"I told him to shut the fuck up and go to bed," he replied. Gino always knew the right thing to say.

CHAPTER THIRTEEN

Turning Japanese

"Art is the illusion of spontaneity."
Japanese Proverb

"*Orakamonos*, you come this way," Shiggy yelled, as he led us down another side street. We were in a city called Kawasaki, not far from Tokyo, and our guide, Shigenori, or Shiggy as we called him, was taking his job seriously, and leading us to a local festival. Hired by our record company, it was his job to be our liaison with our Japanese fans. Earlier that morning, he had arrived at our hotel, obviously excited by the prospect of showing some real American rock n' rollers around his country.

Shiggy was about twenty-five, and wearing dungarees, a Beatles t-shirt, and a Hanshin Tigers baseball cap. The baseball cap was in honor of us being from Boston; it seems that the Hanshin Tigers are thought by many to be the Red Sox of Japanese baseball. They've apparently lost enough big games over the years to earn the nickname "Hard luck Hanshin." Shiggy thought we would feel a kinship with another team whose excruciatingly painful failures were the stuff of local legend.

"Not win too many years," he said smiling and bowing at us, "just like Boston Red Sox." Remember, this was long before 2004 when the Red Sox began turning things around.

We'd been in Japan for a week, and were still getting accustomed to the different world, but unlike baseball, some things didn't translate easily from one culture to another. Shiggy certainly knew our band name, but he seemed to enjoy calling us Orakamonos, which loosely translated as fools. I wondered if there wasn't some part of the Japanese thought of a fool that went beyond our concepts. And while I was really enjoying the people, and the luxurious experience of being in a foreign country, much of the last week had been ego-deflating for me.

We landed in Tokyo to find that, not only did we have a borderline hit in 'Psycho Chicken,' but we also developed a cult following. It's long been known in rock band circles that blond rockers are like Spanish Fly to the Japanese, and we had three, Stacey, Chris, and Rich, and Rich was a redhead who was only temporarily dabbling in a blond color. I saw how things were going to go when we held a press conference the day after we landed; all of the questions were directed at our three blond guys.

Female interviewer to Chris: "Hello, beautiful hair of gold, how are you enjoying our country?"

Chris to female interviewer: "I like it." Squeals of joy and wonder from the assembled press follow this bold announcement. Chris looked confused but happy.

Female interviewer to Stacey: "Hello hair of glowing sun, what do you think of Japanese food?"

Stacey to female interviewer: "I like it." More squeals of joy and wonder; the Pedrick brothers are two for two. Stacey began wondering about Japanese immigration laws; maybe this was the country for him.

Female interviewer to Rich: "Hello glorious red sun that has now turned yellow, what do you know about our country?"

"It's um, pretty cool," Rich responded to more squeals of delight. Doug, at this point has had enough of being ignored, and before Rich could deliver some inane but delight inducing answer, he yelled out, "You lost the war!"

"Holy shit," I was thinking, "now you've done it."

The audience of Japanese rock press sat for a moment in silence, and then, as if on cue, they acted as if they'd just heard the funniest joke since creation. We all learned our Japanese nicknames that day. Chris, Stacey, and Rich, found out that they were collectively called *sanban kinpatsu* no otoko; the blond men. Doug was called *okashii* no hito, or the funny man. And I was called *ta no Hito*...which basically means "The Other Guy."

Shiggy walked quickly ahead of us, waiting at each corner for us to catch up, before he continued. Now he stopped to talk to three young women with cameras that were looking towards us. I knew what was coming.

"Ta No," he yelled to me, "you come, bring *Hagi*." *Hagi* was short for *Hageatama*, which is what Gino was called. It meant "bald one." The Japanese were fascinated by Gino, who in this cultural context, looked like a larger than life Buddha. When we walked the streets of Japan, people would stop, bow towards him and allow us to pass. Gino was as unfazed by this as if he were leading us through a crowded backstage area, but he looked more like a visiting emperor.

"Come on, *Hagi*," I said to him, "your public awaits." Gino smiled and walked over to the awe struck group of bouncing young women. The women handed Shiggy a camera, he turned and handed it to me and inserted himself, arm in arm, among the women and Gino.

"Everyone say *Hagiiiiii*," he yelled, and I snapped the picture. Then I took a picture of the women with The Blond Men and Shiggy, and then another of Gino, The Blond Men and Shiggy. Doug had bought some *yakitori*, or grilled chicken on a stick, from a street vendor and stood patiently eating until we were ready to resume our walk. Finally, Shiggy stopped a passing tourist and we were all included in a group shot.

The Japanese have an amazing ability to pose for photos, I know this because I have photo albums filled with band shots that were never used because someone had either closed their eyes or looked down at the wrong time. But the Japanese are so hip to "the vital moment" that an entire party of boisterous Japanese will immediately snap to attention for a picture. You could probably stop all foot and vehicle traffic in the city of Tokyo for a second, if you could yell CHEESE loud enough. The whole city would turn your way and smile for the picture, and not one person will have blinked at the wrong time.

By now, our walking had brought us to a much more crowded area of the city, and Shiggy still hadn't told us where we were going; he'd said only that we were going to see a street festival.

"Orakamonos, we are almost here," Shiggy said ambiguously, and we all rounded a corner to see quite an amazing sight.

In the center of a city square, on top of a portable shrine, there stood a giant pink penis, easily eight feet tall. All around the square were vendors, selling penis shaped lollypops, penis shaped vegetables, and penis shaped cookies. There were also rows of large wooden

penises (penii?) sticking up from the ground like cannons, and people of both sexes, young and old, would sit astride them and get their picture taken. Shiggy was laughing at the look on our faces as he explained that this was a Japanese fertility festival, dating back hundreds of years, called *Kanamara Matsuri*.

"It means 'Festival of the Steel Phallus,' and people come from all over Japan to touch the big pink penis. We believe it brings us good luck."

Doug was stammering and making odd noises, as if all the jokes that were lined up in his mouth, trying to get out, were crashing into each other. For the rest of the day, we wandered about watching Japanese tourists of all ages sucking little cock shaped candy, and lining up to touch the big pink penis.

It occurred to me that much of the Far East culture remains obsessed with many things having to do with fertility, and all things called aphrodisiacs. It's not just powdered white rhino horns and smoked baby tiger testicles that excite the possibility of lust, the list goes on. In China, drinking a cup of cobra blood is said to heighten sensual awareness, though who knows what the mortality rate is in acquiring it. Older Korean men still eat something called a slime eel, so named because it secretes a stinky mucous when agitated. The trick is to broil it in sesame oil and down it with a shot of liquor. By the way, I know some culinary types who would eat horse crap if that was the procedure.

But it gets scarier; the Japanese pay huge amounts and put their lives at risk to sample the Fugu blowfish; a fish that possesses enough deadly toxins to wipe out an entire wedding party. If cooked properly, and who doesn't trust every chef they've ever met, it is said to produce once again, a heightened sensual awareness. The weird thing is, this part of the planet already has about four billion people so lack of procreating has never been an issue.

The dichotomy might be as simple as this; in old school, family oriented countries, nudity and sexuality are things that are kept in house, and behind closed doors. On the other hand, public fertility festivals, with their ancient beginnings, allow everyone to feel at one with their humanity in a no blame situation; we are simply doing what our ancestors have done before us, so pardon us if we giggle.

I've heard that same giggle from groups of friends when we sat down to a meal of Wellfleet oysters, and someone mentioned the power of oysters. It must also be said however, that if there were some tiny surviving colony of three toed spotted yaks, an Asian herbalist would hunt them down, powder them, and claim them to be the best aphrodisiac of all time.

We collectively got a kick out of the festival and of course there were more pictures taken with the Kinpatsu No Otoko, Shiggy, young girls and big wooden penises. Nowhere other than maybe San Francisco, Key West or Provincetown on Cape Cod would you find that much adoration to the male organ and then in that case, it would be for totally different reasons.

We played a few small shows while we were in Japan, but it was mostly a promotional endeavor. You go where they are playing you, and to that end, we visited more than a couple of radio stations that were playing our song. Japanese pop radio was not much different than American pop radio; a fast talking DJ trying to keep the energy up, and asking stupid questions.

It was at one of these stations that I crossed the line that defines the meat eaters from the salad eaters. The DJ asked me some simple question that had to do with my involvement with Stacey, and perhaps because I was irritated at still another question about a "golden one," I said something flip like, "he's blind in one eye and suffers from flatulence." We in the studio had a laugh about this, but perhaps the translated joke didn't travel well. At our next show, there were people in the audience who were obviously Stacey fans wearing gasmasks and eye patches.

Once I realized that the Japanese rock media would repeat or translate anything I said, I could feel the horns growing on my head. I told them that Rich had been married three times and was an idolater (hey…it sounded bad when they used it in the Bible).

I told them that Chris, oddly enough, collected petrified mammoth droppings. The more they asked, the more I lied, until I realized that I was telling contradictory stories to many of the same people; and yet, much like media everywhere, they repeated all of it.

After about ten days of this nonsense, we were back at the airport getting ready to board a plane for LA, and Shiggy was there to send us off. He had gifts for all of us, and many pictures were taken. I was given a Hanshin Tigers baseball hat and Rich was given three gifts of magic oil, one for each of his wives.

Oddly Chris received a large penis statue made from petrified mammoth droppings which to this day he proudly displays in his back yard. Gino and Shiggy shook hands and bowed to each other.

"Shiggy, you're a good shit," Gino said. Shiggy beamed as if Buddha himself had said it. With that we boarded the plane, and endless drinks and bags of peanuts later, we were back on our home turf.

I always hoped we'd get another chance to go back to Japan and play some of the bigger venues; much like Cheap Trick live at Budokan.

Unfortunately it never worked out and the band didn't get another opportunity to play for our fans. Hopefully they haven't forgotten us though. Even in the few short days we were in Japan, hundreds if not thousands of photos were taken. Middle-aged Japanese women have faded pictures of sanban *kinpatsu no otoko*, Shiggy and Gino to go with stories of the time they met the famous band *Orakamonos*.

CHAPTER FOURTEEN

You're a Peon Tour

"Bonjour," Chris said to the waiter, "*je voudrais pour beaucoup alimentaires pour les personnes.*"

The waiter smiled and said something back to Chris. It was our first night in Paris and we were sitting in a French restaurant not far from the Eiffel Tower. We were filled with everything French, wine, bread, and cheese and now Chris was trying out his high school French. He'd said he would order for all of us and Henri, our French record rep, looked on in amusement, ready to help out but not wanting to interfere.

"You just told him that you would like to support many people," Henri said quietly to Chris. "He said that was noble of you, and then asked if you would like to order some food."

Chris looked more determined and was not ready to give up; two years of high school French must count for something. Another conversation ensued between Chris and our waiter. When it ended, all the plates were removed from the table except for those in front of Chris, and the waiter was now looking at the menu, as if trying to imagine what Chris wanted.

"What happened?" Chris asked Henri.

"I think you told him that food is a good suitcase. He asked if your friends would not be eating, and I think you said that your friends would like you to eat a good suitcase for them."

"Vous etes an dumb ass," Doug said to Chris.

While this was all very entertaining, we were getting hungrier by the moment, so Henri took over and soon we were eating, drinking and discussing our upcoming itinerary. We would spend a week in Paris during which we would appear on two TV shows, lip syncing our songs, and, strangely enough, we would also lip sync a song to a live audience for a radio show. Why would you lip sync a song to a live radio audience that knows you're not really playing you ask? Who can say, but don't argue with the French about these kinds of things; it will get you nowhere.

Unlike many Americans, I found these French idiosyncrasies to be entertaining and endearing; in my view we need eccentric, offbeat, and style conscious countries like France to remind us that life is not all about war and business. I applaud most everything funky, offbeat, obstinate and stylistic about France, and the people I've met are friendly and fun. But the best thing about France, and I know this will sound stupid, it really feels like a foreign country, not just another place trying to emulate America.

Rich Bartlett and I have traveled widely (and wildly) and seen the world in all its many crazy colors. We once sat in a tough back street bar in

Liverpool and wondered at the concept of the world's view of tough guys, knowing full well that neither of us would ever physically qualify in that ranking.

The conversation went something like this; if you had to pick five guys from a bar to fight any other five guys from a bar, from any place in the world, who would you pick?

We grew up in Greater Boston and we've seen Boston and Canadian hockey fans go at it after yet another raucous game between their two respective teams. That led me to say I would take five guys in a bar in either South Boston or Montreal against almost anyone, with Aussie sailors and Brit soccer hooligans coming in a close second. And even though we've been in a few French bars, it never occurred to us to include that country in the conversation. Maybe that's not a bad thing.

We had a wonderfully blurry week in Paris, but by the time we got to lip syncing the radio show, we'd temporarily had our fill with that form of entertainment. My memory of that show is, of course, blurry, but I do remember standing about two feet away from the microphone and using my hand, like a puppet to sing the words to 'It's a Night for Beautiful Girls.' I can't remember whether the attending two hundred people in the audience thought it was funny or not, but let's just say that they did.

The next week or so was hectic, but not because we were playing any gigs; for the most part our

The French 45 release

first trip to Europe was promotional, no road crew, no Gino, just us doing TV and radio shows, and communing with the European rock press.

Each country's rock mags seemed to have their own unique agenda. A French interviewer wanted to know how familiar we were with French performers (is anyone?) and whether people in the band spoke their language; we happily pointed to Chris.

A German interviewer wanted to know if any of us had strong political opinions and I babbled something inane about rock n' roll being a tribal connection between people of all persuasions.

The Brits had nothing to ask us; though we were getting airplay all over Europe, we hadn't been able to crack the edgy, "if you want airplay, you should slash your wrists, shit in your hat and wear it onstage, because then you have a slight chance" world of early eighties British pop radio.

Considering the live shows we were doing at the time, which included nudity, wrist slashing, people screwing sheep, people dressed like nuns and people dressed like nuns screwing sheep, maybe shitting in my hat wasn't too far a leap, but I would certainly have drawn the line at wearing that shit filled hat onstage. A man must know his limits.

In all honesty, I'm not surprised that our stuff didn't get played in England. To the hardcores, we must have seemed light and silly, and to the pop crowd we maybe didn't seem as gay as George Michael or Boy George.

Some other things happened during our first trip to Europe:

We all climbed the Eiffel Tower, and Chris and I bought not only Eiffel Tower shaped bottles of really bad brandy, but other bottles of mind numbing pear brandy whose main feature was that a pear was grown into the bottle, and then it was filled with alcohol. This was like magic to us folk from Ipswich; we were like, "how could they have gotten a full grown pear into that bottle?" You'd think we never saw a ship in a bottle growing up in a coastal New England town.

We landed early one morning in Vienna to find that we were number four on the Austrian charts. There was a press conference which included questions from the local morning TV news, and before the day was over, we had climbed to number one with a bullet on the charts. From this we learned that small countries with rock stations are cool.

One thing we noticed on this trip was that the *Current Affair* types of TV shows were airing rock band videos on a regular basis. The European branch of our record company decided that since 'Psycho

Chicken' was getting a lot of airplay, we should make a video of it. This was the difference between how we were sold in both parts of the world; in America 'Psycho' was deliberately swept under a carpet, but in Europe it was embraced. So off we went to Brussels, where we spent a day at an enormous chicken farm shooting a video. It was great fun, in part because the director didn't speak much English and we didn't speak much French, and therefore much of the communication involved pantomime and bad translations of simple phrases.

At one point the frustrated director, when trying to tell me to pick up a chicken, yelled, "Touch the cock!" I of course couldn't resist grabbing my crotch. Somehow after much laughing and goofing, we got the video done and it was quickly edited and shown all over Europe. This was still a few years before MTV premiered in America and videos became part of every band's bag of tricks.

We did a bit more lip syncing on some German TV shows, and while this lip syncing thing was getting old, we got to meet and hang with some rock legends.

One show in particular, a weekly music show called *RockPop*, seemed to have consistently star studded extravaganzas. The week we were on, the theme was the Old and the New. We, of course, were the New. The Old were people like Donovan, who in person was every bit the friendly, hippie troubadour that you would imagine him to be, and two of my favorite singers from the sixties British Invasion period; Eric Burden of The Animals, and Paul Jones of Manfred Mann. It's sometimes hard to meet your heroes, but both guys were refreshingly normal and friendly.

Three American bands that were becoming hugely popular, Cheap Trick, Foreigner, and Journey also did songs on the show. During the afternoon rehearsals, over German beer and sausages, we all talked about where we were going and where we'd been. It turned out that we would all be attending the following week's three day music-fest in Venice, Italy (more on that later).

My dad spent thirty-three months in Europe and North Africa during WWII, from Omaha Beach on D-Day, to the Battle of the Bulge and on into Germany in the closing days of the war. It was weird to be traveling through some of the same places he'd been to almost forty years earlier, and doing it for something as frivolous as rock n' roll; but engaging in international frivolity is certainly one of the benefits of a generally peaceful world. Thanks, Dad! Just before we left for Europe I asked him if I should bring anything with me. He thought a minute and then said, "Candy and nylons."

In 1980, there were only two (gasp!) TV stations in Spain, and they were both state owned. You'd think that countries with total control of the media would be nervous about having overtly subversive bands singing songs about poultry, and yet there we were, just minutes away from taping our TV segment. Since the studios were outside of Madrid, on days when shows were being taped tour buses filled with tourists would deliver the live audiences. The studio complex was huge, and depending on the day, an audience might get to see a cooking show, a variety show, or a music show.

I think it was Cheap Trick who went on before us and played a couple of songs to an audience of about three hundred; the crowd mostly being made up of teens and young adults.

As you can imagine, the audience loved them and made lots of noise before, during and after their songs. They left the stage, and we were told that there'd be a five minute break, so that the next group of tourists could come in before we got up and played. This was going to be great! We took our places on stage, and watched as the first audience of young people filed out of a side door, and another audience, made up almost entirely of middle aged and elderly nuns, filed in to take their place.

"Is this a fucking joke?" Doug muttered, as the almost entirely black and white clad audience came in and sat down. Richie was giving me the suspicious look he saved for when he thinks I've set something up. Chris, sitting back on the drums, was laughing and saying, "This is perfect."

The odd thing was, that it was perfect, but only if you appreciate the occasional humorous roll of life's dice. As it turns out, one of the characters I would sometimes dress up as was a nun, Sister Fifi Latrine. Then we'd start playing Muddy Waters' great classic 'I'm a Man.' But the words would come out, "I'm a Nun, that's spelled N...U...N...Nun." I'd rewritten the lyrics to reflect the life of a hard drinking, sex and

party loving nun, or as I said in the song, "a natural born lover nun." And now, as if to taunt me with a reprisal, life had given me three hundred elderly nuns in place of the rock n' roll loving youngsters that had been there only moments before. If I was a religious man, I would have bowed down to the classic karma of this moment, but like Chris, all I could do was laugh.

Stacey too was digging the crazy irony. He

smiled and said," You had to dress up like a nun," as if that explained everything.

The sound and camera techs waited a second while we gathered ourselves, and then we began playing 'Psycho Chicken,' a meaningless, goofy, nit witty, song filled with barnyard noises and clucked profanity to a crowd of Spanish speaking old women, who were probably only there hoping to see a cooking show.

We finished the song to polite but steady applause; these poor people from the convent were obviously starved for entertainment. We went right into our second song 'Night Out.'

When that song finished, we gave the crowd a wave and left the stage to a surprisingly loud and enthusiastic applause. Performers were also expected to sign autographs, so we headed out to the ante room expecting nothing, but these women were in for the long haul; and there was a respectable line of about forty old nuns, some with canes, and others in wheel chairs, waiting for us to sign their programs. Maybe at long last, we'd found our crowd.

I sent Peter a telegram the next day that may have made him feel ill at ease. It went something like this: PETER...SPAIN WENT WELL... THREE HUNDRED NUNS CAME TO SEE US PLAY... THEY LOVED US...LOOK INTO BOOKING A SUMMER CONVENT TOUR...GOD BLESS YOU...AND MAY GOD HAVE MERCY ON

YOUR SOUL...YOUR BROTHER IN THE LORD OUR GOD, MIKE.

A week later we found ourselves in Venice, Italy; our month long Euro trip culminating in the band taking part in a three day music fest to be broadcast live on Italian TV.

We were met at Marco Polo Airport by a young Italian man, wearing sunglasses, a light gray suit and an open collared white shirt, and carrying a large homemade sign which in bright colors said *THE FOOLS*. As he helped us carry our bags, and began moving through the crowd, he kept up a running dialogue with few breaths in between.

"My name is Alessio, it means defender, and I'm going to defend you from all those crazy Italian women that will try to suck your rock star cocks. The city is filled with rock stars, everyone is excited. Does anyone get seasick? No? Good, I have a taxi outside that will take us to the hotel. It's the best hotel around. Then we will get drinks and eat. Someday I will come to Boston and you will show me everything, but now it is my turn to show you Venezia! I'm going to quote, show you a great fucking time!"

As he never said "unquote," I tended to think of everything he said from that moment on as being in quotations, but that's just me, and anyhow, it also works in our present format.

We traveled by water taxi to our hotel, a

beautiful, classic, old European edifice overlooking the Adriatic Sea, called The Excelsior. It was gorgeous, with vaulted ceilings and lavish decorations, and in no time we'd had our bags taken to our respective rooms, and we were joining Alessio at a table on the patio near the outside bar, overlooking the ocean. Over drinks, Alessio gave us a quick history lesson about Venice.

"Yes, it's sinking," he said, "it used to sink about three inches a century, but last century it sank almost ten inches, so we better hurry up and finish our drinks! Ha! Don't worry about it; it's been sinking for a thousand years. Look at the ass of that woman over there."

It was late afternoon, and the outside tables were filling up with tourists, rock n' rollers and general show biz types. The music festival, scheduled to start that afternoon, had brought in people and entertainers from all over Europe. The people running it had apparently decided on a broad based view of music.

Hotel Excelsior in Venice

My memory is a little fuzzy on the extensive lineup of performers, but aside from the recent cast of characters we'd been playing with like Journey, Cheap Trick, Donovan, Eric Burden and The Pointer Sisters, there was also Genesis, Billy Squier, Eric Carmen, and a seminal French rocker named Johnny Hallyday, who was known as "The French Elvis." There were dozens of other performers which included Italian opera singers, German rock bands, German country- western bands, Lithuanian folk singers, Austrian yodelers, and even a friggin' Polish polka band. It was the strangest musical concoction I'd ever been a part of and it was a total blast.

Over the next three days, according to a well kept schedule, performers were shuttled back and forth, from hotels to the concert hall, where three large stages were set up. Most bands were only playing one or two songs, and as soon as they were done, the camera would move on to the next stage where another performer was ready to go, and then on the third stage and so on back to the first, so that the hall was in a constant flurry of activity; bands quickly setting up, playing their stuff, and then tearing down to let other bands set up and do the same.

Amazingly, this schedule held together, ten hours a day, for three days, with hardly any mishaps, and it was nationally televised as is. It didn't hurt that some organizational genius decided to space out the rock bands from the individual singers, so that some transitions were made easier. But this nod to practicality also made the artist groupings seem even more eclectic; for instance, a band like Journey would follow a German folk singer duo, and be followed in turn by an Italian opera star. It made for some interesting TV.

We learned that our performance was at six in the evening of the second day. This was an excellent time slot; we could do some sightseeing during the day and since we were only playing one song, by the time we got back to the hotel, we'd be ready for a night of partying.

That first night was spent eating, drinking, and meeting some of the other people staying at our hotel. Cheap Trick, Genesis, a German punk band, and a group of Austrian yodelers were some of the people we hung out with in the spacious bar. Doug, Stacey, and I were drinking with a couple of Brits, one of them a roadie, and one of them may or may not have been Phil Collins. I know you're thinking, what do you mean may or may not have been? It's just that, we weren't all walking around introducing ourselves to each other; it was mostly first names and the assumption was that if you were at the hotel, you were in a band. Also, this was before MTV was everywhere, in every city, and many of the players in even the big, well known bands were able to walk around in relative anonymity.

My memory of the first night is sketchy at best, but I think that, after drinks, we must have all heard that there was a seafood buffet out on the veranda. I seem to recall shrimp, mussels, lobster, crab and various excellent seafood preparations.

We were all quite hammered, but I vaguely remember that the wide display of seafood was set in array around a very large and lifelike wax fish. We thought at first that it was made of ice, as is often the custom in these types of situations, but after one of us poked it the game was afoot.

"Blargly yar umare etsfish," said the man next to me, who might have been the drunken Brit roadie we were hanging out with. He was pointing at the wax fish as if it were an affront to nature.

"Bleesly blag blag," I said in agreement. Stacey nodded. "Garble des sleely?" Doug asked Rich, who was thinking this question over.

"No!" the other Brit said next to me, who may or may not have been Phil Collins, and who had just spoken the first comprehensible word by any of us in minutes. "Blookle bla gah blastoos," he continued; leaving that tiny moment of total communication behind.

He was pointing at the fish and giving us all a conspiratorial wink. Over the next few minutes we miraculously comprehended enough of each other's garble to concoct a plan that had us stealing the fish and taking it to my room. Beyond that, the plan had not developed. You must understand that this very hotel had been used in an early James Bond film, and we were feeling the secret agent moment.

The first step of our drunken plan was an attempted distraction; the Brit roadie was supposed to walk toward the ocean and start yelling, while pointing at the sea. Who knows, maybe there was a shark out there, or worse yet, a drowning hotel patron.

The plan worked almost too well; the roadie's yelling and arm waving attracted not only the life guard, but hotel security. In the ensuing mess, that had him tied up and carried off kicking and screaming, we made off with the fish; without a backward glance at our sacrificed companion.

Such is the lot of rock roadies, who continue to unceasingly give up their lives up for us rockers... there should be an Arlington type cemetery, adjacent to all those glitzy Hard Rock clubs, for these unsung heroes.

When we got the fish to my room, there was disagreement as to what should happen next. Some thought we should throw it out the window. Others thought we should leave it in somebody's bed for the chambermaid. Since we couldn't decide on what to do, we put it in the bath tub and called room service for more drinks, while we sat down to watch TV. At some point someone must have turned on the hot water in the tub, because the next moment of recognition had us all standing around the tub looking at a large mass of generally fish shaped, but melting wax.

This, for some reason, brought about the first

real moment of quasi-panic. Since we were too drunk to take the moment entirely seriously, we did what half wits would do; we hauled the mass of wet wax to my bed and tried to reform it. Unfortunately we were not all on the same page. While one of us was trying to reshape a tail, another of us was trying to form a mustache on the fish's upper lip, and what used to be fins, now were great misshapen wings. And do fish have large antennae? This one did. One of my band mates who shall remain anonymous suggested we mold the fish into a giant penis; undoubtedly thinking back to our trip to the fertility festival in Japan.

When we'd finally had our complete and total way with the poor wax representation, it was well into the wee hours of the morning, and there was no one for us to evade while bringing it back to the patio bar. We put it back on the table we'd taken it from, added some seaweed and shells for good measure, and left the hideous monster there for the morning staff to find.

The last time that I saw the person, who may or may not have been Phil Collins, we were all laughing and stumbling on our way back to our rooms. I've since found out while researching on the web that Peter Gabriel was definitely there during the week in question, and Phil at that point in time, still occasionally played with him. But maybe it wasn't Phil, only he knows.

We learned the next day that Chris and Robin

Zander from Cheap Trick (maybe one of the best pure singers that pop music has ever known), started drinking, talking sports, rock, and life, and had partied till the bar closed.

Looking for a place to continue their talk, Chris remembered that he had a fine bottle of French brandy that had a pear stuck in it. They went back to his room, broke open the bottle and finished it. Chris now remembers this as the worst hangover of his life. The next morning Chris awoke to a painful pounding on his door. It was Cheap Trick's road manager. Robin was not answering his door, and someone remembered him and Chris getting gassed at the bar.

"Do you know where Robin is?" the worried road manager asked.

Chris, head ready to explode and blinded by the light coming through the door, answered honestly based on how he himself felt. "He's probably dead."

Thus ended our first European trip. We left behind the pear brandy, Chris' bad French, lip

Touch the Cock!

synching, German pop shows, nuns, wax fish and people who may or may not have been Phil Collins, and headed back to America. It was time to start work on the second album, but we didn't feel quite ready.

CHAPTER FIFTEEN

What mortals these Fools be.

·

"The music business is a cruel and shallow money trench, a long plastic hallway where thieves and pimps run free, and good men die like dogs. There's also a negative side."

Hunter S. Thompson

"I think you hooked it," Chris said as my drive leaped out into the San Fernando Valley. It was about two in the morning and we were blasting golf balls from the parking lot above the three story condo complex where we currently lived.

Our golf skills being what they were, we had no real chance of hitting anything important, but we were aiming for a water tower about halfway down the slope leading into the valley; it was about two hundred yards away. Even though the Valley was lit up like a neon beehive, as soon as the ball left the club, we lost sight of it. Then we heard a loud *KONG*, which told us that the target had been hit. So far, out of thirty or so drives, we'd only heard that sound a few times, so we celebrated with a beer and a joint.

We'd been in L.A. for a couple of months recording our second album, and we were bored. On this night, Stacey was overdubbing some guitar tracks at the studio, and Rich, as always, was overseeing the project.

That left Chris, Doug, and me to get into whatever trouble we could find, and we'd found a bag of golf clubs and a bucket of balls in a previously unexplored closet in one of our spacious condos. It must have been left behind by a past tenet. In L.A. this kind of thing is more common than you might think; this is, after all, where an inordinate number of people come to get their dreams crushed like mice in a blender. They lay it all on the line for some imagined future of fame and fortune and before they know it, they're skipping out on their rent like thieves in the night and forgetting their golf clubs. Then a drunken rock band moves in and the circle of life continues.

"What's the difference between a hook and a slice?" I asked as Chris stepped up to take his turn. The record company had rented the upper two condos in the building and this was our home base until the record was done. We weren't far from finished, and it wasn't going well.

For the first time in my life I felt no connection with the music I was singing, even though I'd written half of it. The stuff we were creating sounded dark and desperate, and I was already distancing myself from it by only going to the studio when I was needed to sing. While the ten months since our first album had been exciting, we were now suffering the hangover of a complicated cocktail, whose ingredients included:

1. We'd had no time to write, and had no

experience at writing on the road, and so, for the most part, we didn't.

2. We were feeling continued pressure from both our management and EMI to leave our quirky, comedic roots behind and write some friggin' hits. With this new album, we succeeded at the first, but not the second.

3. Our producer, a music legend named Vini Poncia, might have been the perfect guy for us if we had any tunes at all...we didn't.

4. I forget what number four was, but it probably wasn't any good either.

"I think a hook goes left and a slice goes right," Doug said, sipping a beer and sitting in a lawn chair that he'd found two levels below in a hall. A loud *KONG* echoed as Chris' shot also nailed the water tower. We were finding our range; another five hundred thousand or so hits and we'd bring that fucking tower to its knees. A bright blinking light caught my attention coming up the road that led to our condo; this wasn't good.

"Okay people," Chris announced, "we have a cop car making its way into our area-maybe we should *amscray*."

I thought it was very cool that Chris would speak in pig Latin at a moment like this. For some reason, I also thought it was important that we not leave the clubs behind, so while Doug did the right thing and amscrayed quickly through the door on the roof that lead back into the building, I wasted precious moments gathering golf clubs and stray balls. Chris was caught between running to the door and helping a fellow Fool gather evidence; he swore loudly, laughed, and headed back to help me, knowing we were both doomed.

The cruiser came up the side ramp of the building as if this was the last chance to keep the free world safe from stoned tower KONGing golfers, and spun to a stop at the top of the ramp. There were only four cars parked in the spacious lot, and Chris and I were behind two of them. Looking under the car I was hiding behind, I could see the feet of one of the cops as he got out of his car.

"They know we're here," I whispered to Chris.

"So do we," Chris replied.

I found his answer to be so entirely incomprehensible that I began to giggle, and he followed suit. The cops must have heard it and they started walking towards us. At this point I did something that only the truly wild and stupid do; I stood up, made as if I was fumbling with my car keys, and said, "Good evening officers, how can I help you?"

Chris, now nearly convulsed in laughter, was making odd gurgling and whimpering noises. Neither cop slowed down even a half step. One of them replied "You can lie face down on the ground with your hands behind your head. And I want the fuck stick laughing behind the car to do the same."

Chris crawled out from behind the car, the term "fuck stick" being the final straw that closed his home made coffin. He was now laughing too helplessly to take anything seriously, even jail time.

I joined him on the ground and found that yes, this was pretty fucking funny, and soon I too was almost unable to breath from laughing. Somehow even the probability that we were about to be beaten to death by L.A.'s finest, did not cool our jets. The cops waited. We began to take deep breaths. We were going to be alright.

Within a short time, questions were asked and answered and the cops quickly realized that we were harmless rock n' roll goofs who lived one story down from the parking lot. One of the officers, apparently a golfer, took the clubs from us and placed them in the trunk of the cruiser. We were then ordered to return to our condo and cause no more trouble that night.

Aside from a trip to Disneyland, and making a bad album, one other thing of note happened in this general time period: we made another rock video.

At the time we made it, MTV was still six months away from being born, but as we learned from making the 'Psycho Chicken' video in Brussels, it wasn't uncommon for European television to occasionally play rock videos. So it was with more of a nod in that direction that we made a video of Roy Orbison's great classic, 'Running Scared' in February of '81 at a rented bar in East L.A.

The song was never supposed to be on our second album, Heavy Mental, and it was only after we played it as a warm up in the studio that it was added. Vini, who had written songs for as disparate a clientele as The Ronettes, Ringo Starr, Cher, and KISS, probably thought that since we hadn't written an obvious single, why not add a classic and see what happens.

Peter was a bit shocked when he found that we'd recorded the song, but it sounded good enough to keep. We were all surprised when EMI chose the song for the album's single. Our version was faithful, if uninspired, to Roy's original, and there was hope among us that we could get Roy to make a cameo appearance in the video. Calls were made to Roy's people, and EMI was told that it would cost them $25,000. They refused, even though like everything else that was done by them in our name, it was we who'd eventually pay for it. We thought they should pay him; because like the old saying goes-in for a penny, in for a pound(ing). We were already living in a system of indentured servitude to EMI, an enormous company that would, over the years, have its accounting practices questioned in some high profile cases.

A few months later, on August 1, 1981, the world saw the birth of MTV. Actually it wasn't the world as some revisionist historians have claimed; it was just New York and three other American cities. As most fans of that era know, the first video officially played at midnight was The Buggles 'Video Killed the Radio Star.' What few know is this: our video of 'Running Scared' was used for about twenty seconds prior to midnight as a kind of test for color and sound.

 Like almost everything we've ever done, that footnote flew under the radar of history. 'Running Scared' got decent airplay on MTV; for though there was nothing very special about our version of the song, the video was well shot and produced by a group of L.A. pros. Hell, they needed us because at the time MTV was not much more than a bunch of Rod Stewart videos of him prancing around in spandex in front of a

fireplace with half naked women.

After making the album and video, we were back in Ipswich readying ourselves for another three week trip to Europe. It seemed that both the French and Germans were buying lots of our first album, and it was our job to go over there and flog them into a frenzy so that when our second album came out, they would be unable to resist the urge to purchase.

This next sentence is hard for me to type, so first I'll try to just say it out loud:

Before we went back to Europe, we *plyered beago*. No that's not it.

Before we went back to Europe, we *flired Geego*. One more time, slowly.

Before we went back to Europe, we *fired Gino*. There, I said it, and somehow even after all these years it's a painful thing to discuss.

Here's how it went down. There continued to be ongoing friction between Peter and Gino; never raised voices, they were both too professional for that, but always a sense that neither one thought the other was in the long term best interests of the band.

We hadn't had Gino along for either our previous trip to Europe or our time spent in L.A., and Peter thought that with an upcoming summer of touring, we should hire a road manager who had more experience. This was mostly bullshit on Peter's part. I think what he wanted was someone to answer only to him. Even though I sensed this, and knew that Gino could handle anything we gave him, I ultimately sided with Peter, who was our connection to EMI and the rest of the rock world. My thinking was that Peter must know best. Looking back, I was more wrong about Peter than I was about Gino.

The question now came down to who would do the firing. We were scheduled to leave for Europe in two days and Peter said he would do it, but since I knew he cared nothing for Gino, I said I would do it. I tried calling him the day before we were to leave to set up a meeting, but he was out. His girlfriend, Debby, said he was still planning on taking us to the airport in the morning. So that was it; I'd do it on the way out of town.

The next morning we met Gino in a parking lot in Ipswich and piled into his big boat of a car and headed for Logan Airport. He knew something was up, but it took me a while to find my words. I started out saying something about how we needed to make some changes. He knew where it was going and simply said quietly, "You fucking guys."

I told him that we were trying to keep our relationship with Peter from deteriorating, and that this seemed like the right thing to do for the long run. Gino looked at me sadly, like you'd look at a stupid kid, and replied, "Peter doesn't care about you."

There was no way to answer that statement; I knew that Peter did care about us, to the point of distraction from all else that he might have been involved with, but I also knew what Gino meant.

He'd seen us exactly how we were, almost from day one, and his thought was that if you paid attention to what they did, you would understand The Fools. Peter, after hearing our songs and seeing what we could do to a crowd, saw much bigger, arena type visions; visions that had us leaving our humor roots. That view ultimately proved to be ass ended and ignored a basic management tenant; identify your client's strengths and amplify them.

The rest of the ride to the airport was quiet. When we got to the airport and piled out of his car, Gino looked at all of us, shook his head, and said, "Good luck." Then he got back into his big American car and drove off.

I didn't see him again for years, but I heard he found a job as a night watchman for the local nuclear power plant. Gino was always good at watching out for people and we missed him, but the show had to go on…and it did. We didn't know it then, but we were about to *really* miss Gino.

CHAPTER SIXTEEN

The Gripes of Roth

"Don't let the same dog bite you twice."
Chuck Berry
"The worst crime is faking it."
Kurt Cobain

"Come on people try it again!" Our choreographer was doing his best to get us to take his lessons seriously, and this last dance step he'd given us had us bumping into each other and laughing.

"This is not a fucking joke!" he yelled as we started doing deliberately bad imitations of what he'd shown us.

But it *was* a fucking joke; Peter had decided that the best way to get us to open up and take full command of the stage, was to hire David Bowie's choreographer, and rent the 2,800 seat Orpheum in Boston so that we could rehearse there.

If that sounds like it was money that *he* spent, let me remind you once again that it was money that we spent. In retrospect, everything done that week could have been done cheaper or not at all; but the manager/band psychology can often take some painful side trips.

We always thought that we already owned whatever stage we were on, but if someone you've hired to guide you says that what you believe just ain't so, maybe you let your insecurities make the call and agree.

The choreographer's idea of me owning the stage had me entering from stage right, seconds after the opening song started and doing high leg kicks as I made my way to the front of the stage, looking like the lead dork in a high school presentation of *Oklahoma*.

Let's not forget that we were about to head once more into the fucking rock n' roll breach, and we seemed to be armed with swizzle sticks and plastic chickens! It would have made more sense for Peter to organize a week of us shooting drugs, getting tattoos, and banging hookers; in the end, none of that would have helped either, but it might have been less demeaning.

It was around this time period that I finally started to question Peter's vision, or more precisely, I started to question why I didn't have a stronger vision of my own, because blaming someone else for your own lack of direction is like admitting you were blind.

If all we ever wanted was a recording contract, an opportunity to spend money like water, and a chance to look like assholes on stage, we should have been delighted. I honestly don't know if Peter ever thought he had rounded the corner on whipping us lumps of clay into rock star shape, but I do know that mutiny was starting to set in.

And let this be a wag of the cautionary tale for a young band looking for management; try to remember that THESE PEOPLE WORK FOR YOU. IT DOESN'T MATTER THAT YOU HAVEN'T BEEN AROUND, MAKE YOUR OWN DECISIONS, AND MAKE THEM FROM THE HEART!...(ahem)... sorry for yelling...but this stuff is important.

Having said all that, Peter, or someone at EMI, landed us the backup slot on one of the biggest tours of the summer of 1981, the Van Halen *Fair Warning* tour.

Van Halen, during the eighties, would have more top one hundred hits than any other hard rock or metal band, and would go on to become the twentieth bestselling band of all time. The slot was probably Peter's idea of giving us a golden opportunity to make our way onto the arena circuit.

There was however one major problem with this thinking; we had nothing in common with a hard rock pop metal band, we were oceans away; a tight, quirky, little new wave pop band, and our latest single was a remake of a Roy Orbison ballad. No amount of

high leg kicks and choreographed Broadway bullshit on my part would disguise the fact that, while many bands would have driven over baby seals in a bulldozer to get on this tour, for us it was an odd choice.

It might have made more sense for us to work our way around the country playing two thousand-seaters, but I'd be lying (again) if I said I wasn't excited about us going out and playing to fifteen to twenty thousand people every night. Just like a firehouse dog, when the bell rang I was on the bus and ready to roll.

Our first gig with Van Halen was in Moncton, Nova Scotia, the biggest little Canadian city I never heard of prior to this tour, so it was our first close up view of the mega-band we were touring with. This was Van Halen at the height of their powers and our initial impression was that this was going to be a fun tour; bass player Michael Anthony seemed friendly and normal, and Eddie Van Halen couldn't have been nicer. The guitar virtuoso had recently hooked up with actress Valerie Bertinelli, and she came along for parts of the tour.

The fact that an actress who often played "the girl next door" was hanging out with a loud, nasty rock band couldn't help but elevate her babe status in our eyes; but any prurient interest we might have imagined was quickly deflated when we saw Eddie and Val together-they seemed really happy and in love.

Without the internet giving any hack with a camera a byline, the media world was much smaller in 1981, and she was a star on one of the biggest sitcoms before there was widespread cable, and there were only a handful of major networks.

What I'm trying to say is this; anyone who watched TV knew who she was, and since Eddie was a major rock star, the two of them were a definite early eighties celeb power couple. There's no doubt that if today's entertainment media existed back then, these two would have been hounded from coast to coast and given some stupid nickname like Eddval...or Vanelli. As it was, they seemed to be able to travel in relative anonymity, and we saw them out and about more than once.

It was hard not to like seeing them together, and they not only remembered our names but, at times, would engage us in actual conversation. I know you're stunned at this, but it's not unusual behavior for people who are involved in a thirty-six city joint endeavor to act like neighbors. For all I know, Eddie thought our band sucked, but he was a gentleman and weren't we, after all, in this together.

As a performer and guitar player, Eddie seemed to show up fully formed. What I mean is, from the first time you ever heard a Van Halen song on the radio, you were probably thinking, "Who is that guitar player?"

I've always thought of Jeff Beck as being the pinnacle of what a guitar player can do in both power and originality, but the first time I saw Eddie on stage, it was jaw dropping. He was almost like a circus act. He would run to the front of the stage, riffing on his guitar like an assault rifle and the look on his face said that even *he* was amazed at the sounds he was making.

I talked to Stacey about this recently, and we both agreed that, while the Van Halen show was the same every night, right down to what David Lee would say to the audience, when Eddie went off on an extended solo, he never seemed to play it the same way twice.

David Lee Roth on the other hand was a puzzle to us from the start. From our very first encounter, at polar opposite to his good guy, carefree stage persona, he appeared distant, paranoid and intense. While the rest of the band seemed to be dealing pretty evenly with stardom and the fact that they'd be seeing us Fools nightly over the course of the summer, he wanted nothing to do with us in any way; we were simply "the opening guys."

I couldn't figure out what the problem was, but a long time roadie of theirs suggested that maybe because the band had come through the shark infested waters of the LA club scene, and had been kicked in the nuts more than once as a backup band, that David Lee wanted to do the same to his backup bands. This same roadie said this to us: "You guys won't last long, no one does."

Over the years, it's almost become a rock n' roll

parlor game to discuss the merits of the three singers Van Halen employed. Along with David Lee, there were two other very fine vocalists; Sammy Hagar and Gary Cherone, and as a singer, David Lee suffers greatly in comparison with either of the other two, but count me among those who think it's not really Van Halen without David Lee.

His pomp, bluster, and big show sensibility places him in a place all his own amongst the great pop metal singers of all time. And yet, of all the bands we ever played with, he ranks a clear number one on the treated us like shit list. From almost day one, messages were sent back to us from David Lee, messages that his little, rat prick Nazi of a road manager seemed to delight in delivering.

"No more jumping off the drum riser," he would smile and say, "David Lee does that."

We, of course, would comply, but then after another week or so, the next message was delivered.

"Don't walk back and forth across the stage, David Lee does that. Do it again and you're off the tour."

Once again I complied, because, after all, our whole summer was locked into us doing this tour. But before long our pre-show deli platter stopped coming, and we became a stressed out band. More than once I wanted to talk to Eddie about all of this, but every time I saw him, he was with Valerie, and they had little heart shapes in their thought balloons. I kept thinking the whole thing would work itself out. I never missed Gino more; if only because one look from him would have taken the fun out of delivering these messages to us.

At some point, when the creepy road manager came backstage and smiled at our question about pre-show food, the very quick witted Rich Bartlett said,

"Well at least bring us the brown M&M's."

It was well known in rock circles that Van Halen had a rider that had an unusual request in it. A rider is something that a band adds to a contract. It contains items like this:

There will be a hot meal provided for five band members and seven crew members.

There will be a case of beer on ice and a bottle of Stolichnaya vodka.

There will be a full grown live penguin.

Okay, that was our rider, and the reason we said a penguin instead of a monkey was that someone could have actually provided us a monkey since they are much easier to procure.

The deal is that you want to know that concert promoters and their staffs are actually reading your rider, so you put something ridiculous on it.

In Van Halen's case, they said "no brown M&M's." Probably because of their stature, venues actually brought them a huge plate of the candies minus the brown ones. From the day of Rich's smart ass comment onward, a plate of brown M&M's was delivered to our dressing room, in lieu of pre-game food.

There was always a chance that all of this bullshit directed at us came not from David Lee, but his full on, proud to be an asshole, road manager, and since Roth avoided all contact with us, how could I prove otherwise. I can't, but I can offer this anecdote that led me to believe it was David Lee.

Somewhere in the middle of the country and halfway through the tour, I entered our hotel bar and saw him sitting alone and nursing a drink. I thought this will be a perfect time to find out what's up. I sat a stool away and said something like this:

"The band is sounding great, man, how you doin?"

He looked at me and said, "I'm doin' great man, are you going to the show tonight?"

I realized then that even though he was allegedly sending his nasty shit backstage to us nightly, maybe it was indeed as the roadie had said, not personal. David Lee seemed to have no idea who I was. The fact that it was maybe something that he did a lot to many other bands sealed it for me. I think I knew then we were doomed, but I said this anyway, "I have to go to the show tonight; I'm in the opening band."

With that, he looked oddly at me, put his drink down, and left the bar. It was damn weird. Within a week, another message was delivered saying that I wasn't allowed to talk to the audience in between songs, because that's what David Lee does, and this message had a second part to it-quit trying to copy David Lee's moves.

This was the most embarrassing part of the tour for me; the thought that anyone in Van Halen's camp would think I was trying to copy David Lee. Was he just fucking with us, or was he really that insecure? It's not that he wasn't dynamic and even athletic; his favorite move was to jump up and do an in air leg split with his outstretched arms aimed at his feet. It's just that, to me, he couldn't have seemed any more like a high school cheerleader if he had a pompom in each hand.

In actuality, the people I was trying to emulate during that tour were the same people I've been trying to emulate most of my life; some combination of Ray Davies, Peter Wolf, Muddy Waters, and Mick Jagger...perhaps with a little Stan Laurel thrown in. These were the people I was stealing from, not the USC pep squad.

The tour rolled on, from late May, through June and into July, and early on we realized that it made no sense for me to croon out our Orbison single to a metal crowd, so we stopped playing it. But we were doing well, in spite of the hand grenades periodically lobbed backstage.

As a band, we've always looked at shows as wins

or losses, and it's all about how you feel as you're coming offstage. Of the thirty-six cities we did with Van Halen throughout North America, we graded ourselves as thirty-four wins, one loss, and one tie. No one cares about ties, but I'll tell you that the one loss was early on in the tour, a beaten to the knees drubbing in New Jersey where we were roundly and thoroughly booed.

The audience, thus galvanized in their hatred of us, probably enjoyed VH all the more. Sometimes that's the lot of an opening act; warming them up means bringing them together in their hatred for your band to make the headliner all that much more anticipated and loved by the crowd. It can be irritating, but as the French say, that's life.

By July, acting on orders from on high, I wasn't allowed to walk, move, talk, breath or jump on stage…these all being things that David Lee did. In spite of these handcuffs, we went on every night, did our forty minutes, played well, and then hopped on the bus ready to travel to the next show. We'd started the tour heading north and west, across the northern states and Canada, and after heading down the west coast, we made our way back east across the Midwestern and southern states. Now, after more than two months, we were heading up the east coast.

We were excited because we were going to get to play Boston Garden, our first New England show in what seemed like forever. It would be a homecoming for us, but it never happened; a week before Boston we found out we were off the tour.

We were stunned, but we shouldn't have been. If traveling with VH taught us anything, it was that they wiped their asses with opening acts. Maybe someone in the band was mad that all the strictures put upon us hadn't made us quit; this'll show 'em, we'll fire 'em just before we play their hometown. More likely it was the kind of simple casual cruelty that some people deliver just because they can.

You might wonder who took our place; it must have been an up and coming band that has since gone on to make their name in the world. No, I don't remember their name, but I think they were from Philadelphia, and they only did a few dates on the tour after we got kicked off.

We got back to Boston ahead of the tour but the word of our ouster had arrived home before us. Some friends at WBCN wanted to know if we would like to go public with our version of why we were off the tour; maybe do the morning show, the venerable Big Mattress with Charles Laquidara, and talk about it. But there didn't seem to be any way to look good by going public with the mess Van Halen handed us, so we laid low, spent time with our families, and got ready to head back to Europe, a short tour that would take place in a few weeks.

Looking back all these years later, I'm still not sure why all that shit happened on that tour. Could

David Lee have really been so insecure at the height of his popularity that he was somehow bothered by a backup band? I didn't believe it until I heard his radio show; it was embarrassingly bad.

He took radio boorishness to new levels and seemed to really believe that he could take over the public airwaves that radio god Howard Stern once ruled. But the reason Howard changed radio forever is because he was real, and people sensed it. In this case there was no guitar genius to balance David Lee's bullshit and people quickly tired of his radio act when they realized there was no visible person behind the bluster.

Maybe some people can't get enough public adulation. I figure it's pretty much a given that all performers are seeking some form of public self validation, and that it hopefully gets evened out by the love of the music, or the dance, or the acting roles they're playing. If that all gets out of whack, and the results of your art; things like money, adulation, and power become more important than the act of performing, it can get ugly.

It might have been best if we'd gotten out of the way of that ugliness early on and quit the tour, but sometimes you get into a survivor mode and just try to make it to the next day. In the long run, the experience helped us greatly; we got up and played, night after night, under adverse conditions, and let the music pull us through.

In the almost thirty years since that tour, we've done shows not long after broken bones, broken marriages, and family deaths. The music has done for us what it's supposed to do for everyone; it's given us an escape into a healing release. If anything, that's made the trip worth every mile.

The Fools rock 'n' rolled 864,942 people on the Van Halen Tour last year. Now they're ready for you!

THE FOOLS

Agency: William Morris / 1350 Avenue of the Americas, New York, NY 10019 / (212) 586-5100
Record Label: EMI America / 6920 Sunset Boulevard, Los Angeles, CA 90028
Management: Castle Music Productions / 923 Fifth Avenue, Duplex Suite, New York, NY 10021 (212) 772-9335

CHAPTER SEVENTEEN

Playing With House Money

*"I never had the feeling I ever made
a dime doing anything"*
Rick Rubin

*"I'm a survivor in a business that
constantly rejects you."*
Dick Clark

"Tonight at the Channel, we're giving away a car, so if you don't want to miss the chance of winning it, you better be there!" So said I in 1985 on New England's biggest rock station, WBCN in Boston.

We'd bought a junk car that would barely move, and we were taking advantage, and not for the first time mind you, of people's willingness to believe. If you were one of the people there that night, we didn't see it as mean, we saw it as funny. And ultimately, the joke was on us.

The Boston Fire Department demanded that the only way we could have the car brought into the club, was if we had a mechanic remove the gas tank. Add to that the towing charges to and from the club, because of course the person who won the car didn't want it, and it was a reasonably expensive joke. Who came up with this brilliant promotion strategy? I think it was Leo's idea. Who in the hell is Leo you ask? He's our drummer, but I'll get to that in a minute.

The Channel was Boston's biggest rock club. It was listed as a 1,200 capacity, but we had nights there that must have passed 2,000.

It was on the south side of town down by the piers and had kind of a lawless, Wild West atmosphere. Stuart "Dinky" Dawson, a Brit transplant who, as a soundman, had pioneered the whole concept of mixing house sound with seminal bands like The Who and The Byrds, chose The Channel as a place to retire to after years on the road, and held court there nightly after the shows.

The Channel - circa 1985

It was our Boston home for a few years, and there were summer nights when the club actually ran out of beer when we played. Though we consistently packed the place, the Boston press had apparently had enough, and completely ignored us.

EMI dumped us in 1982 after two records that had probably totaled a few hundred thousand in sales, and while today that would be looked on as an impressive start to a career, EMI decided to try to find a quick buck elsewhere. From a local media point of view, we seemed to be people who'd stayed too long at a party; the sound they'd dubbed new wave had mostly come and gone, and how could we still be alive if they didn't decree it so. The "madcap, zany antics" that was once our calling card were now thought of as our drawback.

And yet, while we were trying to get people sold on the "win a car" thing, we also now had another song on the radio, once again given to a station as a cassette, if you can believe it, and once again getting requested to the point of hit status, not only in Boston, but in Worcester, Albany, Houston, and San Francisco. The song was a country thing we came up with while we were backing ourselves up as a band called Mel Smith and his Wild In-laws.

The In-laws started as a joke, what else, during some downtime between tours in the early eighties. We thought it would be funny to back up The Fools and come out as a band from Buttpoke, Tennessee, and play songs like 'Bigfoot Stole my Wife,' and 'She's my Grandma, She's my Mother, She's my Wife.'

Sucked into this batch of nonsense was a tune called 'Life Sucks Then You Die.' It might never have hit the airwaves if an old friend and Boston DJ Carter Alan hadn't come to hear us one night and inquired about the song.

"If you give me a copy of that song, I'll play it," he said.

We did, and he did, and within a few weeks it was being requested to the point where it went into heavy rotation, and was being handed around the country from station to station. This was the third time we had performed this magic trick, and just like the first two, we didn't have a recording contract to take advantage of it…nor were we making any money off of it.

But before we get into all that, it's time to meet the new band members. Okay, I know what you're thinking-"New band members! What the fuck! We were just getting to know the original band members!"

Yes, these things can be hard but you're going to have to understand that rock bands are like marriages, some last and some don't…but because rock bands can be four, five or six partner marriages, the pride of survival with some members, can be negatively balanced by the breakup with others.

Not long after the 1981 Van Halen tour, and shortly before we were to head back to Europe, Chris dove into a tree while playing Frisbee, and broke his collar bone and dislocated his shoulder. There was no chance he could play drums on the Euro tour, so we borrowed Jeff from The Nervous Eaters, and figured we'd see Chris on the other side.

When we got back from Europe, Chris still wasn't ready, and wouldn't be for a while, and it became apparent that it was time to part musical ways. I'd played with Chris for years, even before The Fools, and we'd had countless adventures, so it sucked, and I worried if we'd ever be the same.

Chris, for his part, said this to the local paper about his departure from the band, "I've been to the mountain top, and I know I don't want to live there."

On that same Euro tour we also parted ways with Stacey. It must sound like we were working a pogrom against the Pedrick brothers, but it's a case more of how things shook out. In Stacey's situation it had much to do with stress levels. I know I was feeling stressed and thinking that we should add a keyboard player, hopefully a person who could also write some songs, as Doug and I were not becoming the Lennon-McCartney music factory that Peter and EMI hoped us to be.

The fact that Stacey took the hit might have come down to him being replaceable in our manic self-evaluation as to who did what. It wasn't easy; he and I and Chris had grown up working the Ipswich coal mines together and no amount of rock n' roll bullshit would ever change that.

For a while Jeff from the Eaters played drums for us until it became apparent that we needed to hold a drummer audition. A word now to anyone anywhere that plays in a band and thinks of going the audition route to find a player: Don't do it.

Not only are you dabbling in the murky mind fuck of people's dreams, but you're putting yourself at emotional and perhaps even physical risk. Our three day open audition for drummers was an open season on us. Acknowledging that a painful memory can dim over time, some things still lurk in the dark museum of this time period.

Understand that holding an open audition allows anyone to show up, and that, once they do, you are at least temporarily, the judge and jury on their talent, their personality, and their musical career. About twenty people answered the call to drum for us, and most of them were at least passingly good and/or emotionally fit. Some weren't. I list them for you.

*One guy came in, told us he didn't know anything about us, took out a notebook, and tried to teach us some songs he wrote. He was insulted when we told him to leave.

*Another drummer knew all about us, played pretty well, but thought we'd be better if we lost that "comedy thing." Then, fearing he'd crossed a line, he wouldn't leave until he felt we understood his true devotion to us. He named song after song, as if it might save him. It was uncomfortable.

*At least two drummers came, I think, just to get autographs; they knew they couldn't play well enough to get the gig, but here's a chance to meet The Fools. If you're not of a certain age and from the Boston area, you probably don't understand these last two guys. We did.

*One drummer came in, reeking of pot, and promptly took a huge dump in the bathroom, which quickly wafted out to us in our small rehearsal place, and then spent fifteen minutes adjusting the drums. When we finally started playing, he had this unusual habit…if a song got quieter, he played slower…if a song got louder, he played faster. It was late in the day, and we were probably bored but when we in the band realized this, we investigated the possibilities of his handicap, to the point where we played so quietly, he almost stopped…and so loudly that he almost exploded in his effort to match our volume with unbridled speed. Sadly, I think he thought that he'd finally found his perfect band. What do you say to people like this? "We'll think it over and maybe we'll call you."

Oddly enough, the first guy we auditioned was the best. Who knew that we could have spared ourselves and our auditioners? Not to mention a couple of trees worth of drumsticks and all that pain. His name was Leo Black who you might remember from an earlier chapter; he was one of the people who stormed the party at Castle Hill, and he was convinced he had no shot at drumming for us. But he did what some people do when they want a phone call they don't think they'll get; he took a bath. We called him moments after he climbed into the tub. That was almost thirty years ago. I don't mean to say that he's been in the tub for thirty years, he hasn't, but he's still our drummer.

When Leo joined us in 1981, we still had a contract with EMI. Within a year, that was gone, and within another year, so was Doug. Not that I want to speak for him, but I think Doug, more than Rich and I, felt the imposed weight of our situation. At some point he decided he'd had enough and left to help his wife pursue a country music career.

Now it was down to just the two of us. Rich and I wondered for a bit whether we should even keep the band name, but then I remembered coming back from California years earlier, wanting to start a band, and thinking that getting Rich in the band was job number one. In a sense, while everything else had changed, we were still the nucleus of an idea, and I figured why not keep it breathing?

After Doug's departure, and because we couldn't seem to get enough of a bad process, we held open auditions for a bass player. Leo knew a guy named Joe Holaday who showed up, played everything perfectly, and was obviously a good dude. We could have stopped right then and moved forward with Joe, but no, there were bass players to insult, and be scared by... there were more dreams to shatter, and more bad smells to be experienced. At the end of three days, we were in the same place as when we started; Joe Holaday was by far the best and he became our bass player.

It started to occur to me that perhaps there's some kind of unwritten rule in the musical universe that says the first guy you audition will be the best guy. We certainly were batting a thousand with that.

This new lineup of Rich, Joe, Leo, and me began in 1983 and would remain the same for the next twenty years. We became essentially a power trio with a lead singer.

Though, over time, we tried adding another guitar player, and for a while, a keyboard player, they didn't last, and Stacey was never replaced.

The New Lineup – Joe, Mike, Leo & Rich

Our relationship with our manager Peter had taken some lumps, and we had mostly parted ways with him, but with the success of 'Life Sucks…' we partnered up again and released an album called *World Dance Party*.

Once again, though the road was already paved with much airplay, the major labels shied away from us. We were thought of as loose cannons, and the music of the mid-eighties was hairy, big time, corporate rock. There was nothing funny about it, and anything sounding like a country song had a backwater tinge to it that the records companies avoided like the plague.

Still from the video

Peter though knew we had other options as the biz was starting to change. He brought us to Jem PVC, a New Jersey based company whose name may have sounded like they made plastic pipes, but who actually made and distributed records. Kim Fowley, The Plasmatics, Siouxsie and the Banshees, and Dr. Demento were some of the eclectic acts on the label, and for the first time we felt free to do exactly what we wanted.

World Dance Party not only contained the tunes 'Life Sucks…' and 'She Makes Me Feel Big' but a remake of Manfred Mann's classic, 'Doo Wah

The extras practice their dance moves

Diddy.' We did a video for that song shot in downtown Salem, MA…you know, best known for the place where they burned witches at the stake. No witches or Fools were torched but I still run into people this day who claim they were in the video. I equate that to someone who claims they were at Fenway Park when the great Ted Williams hit his final homerun when the footage clearly shows few people in the park. We had a lot of extras, but not as many as I've met through the years.

The video for 'Doo Wah Diddy' found itself in heavy rotation not only on the New England based video channel called V66 but on MTV; which at the time was the place for all things popular in rock. If you got frequent play on MTV, you'd sell some albums, radio stations would play your stuff and people would pack your shows.

After a few years of spinning our wheels, we were rolling again and to prove it, we rented the Hayden Planetarium at the Museum of Science in Boston and held our record release party there. Our idea was to build a light and laser show around our music with pictures of the band and videos interspersed among the planets.

It was the first time anyone had used the Planetarium for anything like this and it was entirely and totally awesome. This time, unlike our party at the Castle, and in order that nothing get broken, and no planets get stolen, we held strong to a confirmed guest list. We also agreed with Peter that this time, we would not invite the monkey.

"We had a disagreement with EMI, they wanted to get rid of us and we didn't want to go."
- Rich Bartlett, Fool, when asked why The Fools were no longer with EMI.

CHAPTER EIGHTEEN

When in Doubt, Play on

*"You gotta be business savvy really, or else
you get the piss taken out of you."*
Melanie B. Spice Girls

*"I wish there had been a music business
101 course I could have taken."*
Kurt Cobain

After the success of *World Dance Party*, we recorded one more record with Jem in 1987, an evening in front of 2,000 people at The Channel. It was called, *Wake up, it's Alive* and it's a nice little piece of history, not only for us, but for people who have fond memories of the former club.

It sold fairly well, mostly because of a Screamin' Jay Hawkins cover called 'Bite It,' and the folks at Gem seemed happy, but at some point we began to wonder why we couldn't start our own record company. Back then, thinking of releasing anything that wasn't fronted by a large record company wasn't thought of as independent, it was thought of as stupid and desperate.

Today of course with the advances in technology that allow anyone to set up a state of the art recording studio in their basement on a personal computer, the way music is delivered to the masses has evolved and many well-known recording artists are going independent; no longer beholden to the whims or corporate arrogance of a large record company.

Since the beginning of The Fools, we'd developed strong personal relationships with radio stations, not only in New England, but in other parts of the country, and there were regional chains of stores like (the since departed) Strawberries and (the still going strong) Newbury Comics that were willing to accept and stock our products. Going independent felt like a natural fit for us.

Since we were mostly playing in New England, and there was no chance of us getting a sniff of anything national at this point of our career, it finally became apparent that there wasn't really anything for Peter to manage; all we needed was an agent to book us (eventually we would take that over too). In retrospect, Peter did many good things for us, and he put his contacts, his vision, and his credibility all on the line. One of his friends reportedly said to him, "Are you still dragging that horse around?"

As we were coming close to the end of our relationship, I think he finally realized that we only flourished when we were given the freedom to be us. And we began to realize that our idea of "flourishing" had less to do with piles of money than it had to do with mental health, and the feeling that we were our own masters.

For the next few years, into the nineties, we would periodically release an album, and while there were no tunes that garnered much airplay, there were still some stations in New England willing to give us a shot. WBCN hadn't yet entirely sold its soul, and Charles, Marc, and Carter, were people we could count on to play our stuff. Greg Hill (The Hillman) from WAAF was another friend whose long running morning show had us on periodically to promote a show or new record.

Standing out even in this crowd of supporters would have to be WHEB's Greg Kretschmar, the host of The Morning Buzz. This southern New Hampshire show broadcast out of Portsmouth has become a staple in many people's drive to work and Greg and his supporting cast are like extended family.

Greg has a tape of himself, then just a starting out part-time DJ, introducing us at a show in 1984 in which he sounds impossibly young and very excited. He took over the morning show in 1987, and is still going strong twenty-three years later. As he says, that kind of longevity in radio almost qualifies him as a *Jurassic Park* exhibit. We can relate.

By the mid-nineties, our live show was better than ever, and people were beginning to use the phrase "legendary" when they spoke about us. There were even tours given in Ipswich that would take you past our boyhood homes, on the way to Pedrick's Hole and The Clam Box, a now nationally known eatery. Ipswich, no longer a backwater mining town, had achieved its own legendary status, as the go to place for fried clams. Also the revelation that people would pay large amounts of money to go to Cranes Beach, did not hurt the local tourist trade. Life was good all around.

Leo was now handling most band business, and Joe, already a terrific bass player, had become the perfect straight man and announcer for my stage nonsense. It was during this time period that another character surfaced; I would come on stage dressed in a plaid shirt, green hat with earflaps, corn cob pipe, and rubber boots. I had recently become a fan of the rapper LL Cool J, so my character, with a nod towards the world famous Maine store, was a down home rapper named LL Cool Bean. It was the kind of big stupid that we did well.

"I live in Maine that's way up here, I wear hats with flaps on the ears

If you want directions you'd better stay clear, 'cause I'll tell you

You can't get there from here
LL Cool Bean! LL Cool Bean!.......ah yup"

LL Cool Bean

On any given night, to start the show, I also came out as a plumber, a lottery winner, a priest, a nun, and a cowboy. Around this time, Bret Milano, an excellent rock writer for *The Boston Globe*, certainly aware that we were no longer part of the in crowd, mentioned us as a "guilty pleasure." While I'm sure he meant it as a compliment, it came off sounding like we were relegated by the local paper of record to bathroom jerk-off material. But still the people came to our shows in droves, and not one of them was wearing a bag on his head, as if ashamed to be seen there.

Mike naked on stage

The four of us became a

very tight musical outfit, with Rich being somehow able to seamlessly play rhythm and lead at the same time. He has always been a master technician, and I think it's only because we play comedy based rock that he hasn't been nationally recognized.

Every time I see an issue of *Guitar Player*

Rich contemplates a shoe

magazine, and they're featuring a guy who appeared on some hit record, I think of how Rich has gone mostly undiscovered by the critics who rate guitar players. There are members of our fanhood that come to shows just to stand down front and watch him. Honestly, how many guitar players have the style and sensibility to slide effortlessly from rock to country to blues, and nail every classic lick, all the while adding just enough of a slight and deliberate overplay to make it somehow funny and spectacular at the same time? Rich is all by himself in that category.

He has also either mixed or overseen the mix on everything we've ever put out, from day one. Aside from that, and dryly so, he's probably the funniest person in the band, and you heard that from me, a pretty friggin' funny guy myself.

Joe Holaday's playing, melodic, powerful, and

intelligent, was everything a power trio needed to float the boat. When I tell you Joe is a genius, I mean an honest to God Mensa type, and in a world full of idiots, me at times included, he suffers us all gladly. I need to tell you a story that illustrates him perfectly.

In the early years of Joe joining the band, he and I were heading to a show, at The Casbah in Manchester, NH, in a new car that I'd only made one payment on. It was a sunny day in July, and we'd just pulled up to a stop light. I was telling Joe a joke that started like this-"These three guys walk into a bar," and WHAM! we got hit from behind by a young woman in her daddy's Caddy who never saw

us. Joe and I were thrown forward, me breaking the steering wheel, and then whiplashed back so powerfully that our bucket seats snapped and we were flat on our backs into the backseat area, the backseat area that no longer existed; because the end of my car was pushed up to within about six inches from our heads. I looked at Joe to see if he was okay and he calmly said,

"So what did the first guy say?"

In all my years, I don't know if I've ever seen a better example of coolness under fire. He knew we'd almost been killed, but he refused to go there. We jumped out of my car, not knowing anything about the adrenaline rush that shock and damage can give your body, and then not only checked on the girl who hit us, who was fine, we also pushed my car off the road.

When the ambulance came, we talked them out of a trip to the hospital by saying that we played in a band called The Fools and that we were on our way to a gig. One of the medical techs was impressed by this, so after signing an autograph, we called Joe's wife Donna to give us a ride to the show. Since my car had been towed away, she didn't get to see the crushed lump of steel that it had been turned into so she had no idea how seriously we'd been whacked. Besides, we seemed ok and we were very talkative on the way to the gig.

That bogus energy lasted into the third song of the show, at which point I felt an incredible wave of jelly wash through my body. All of the adrenaline left me, and I finished the last twenty songs of the set sitting on the front lip of the stage. Joe looked like I felt; totally washed of anything resembling energy.

After the show Donna drove us home, and when I got to my house, Ginny was waiting up to see how I was doing. This was before the constant available chatter of cell phones, and the last she'd heard from me was the fast talking guy who was "ok" right after the accident. She took one look and knew I was a mess. We went to the hospital in the wee hours of the morning; I received drugs, went home, and couldn't get out of bed for a few weeks. No permanent damage was done to Joe or me, we were soon playing again, and we luckily avoided an obituary that would surely have said that our song 'Life Sucks...Then you Die' was not only ironic, but prophetic.

Joe and I weren't the only ones in the band to suffer band related injury. During a show in the mid-eighties Leo Black once tried jumping down onto his drum stool from a shelf behind the drums and drove a piece of drum hardware a half inch into his shin. He finished the show in a pool of blood and couldn't play for weeks after.

Also he was never blessed with a strong back, and the very nature of sitting down and pounding the drums can take its toll on the spinal cord of even a casual drummer. Periodically over the years, and sometimes for a year or two at a time, he's found it necessary to stop playing the drums. Each time that it's happened, we feel we've played with him for the last time, but every time he heals enough to play again, he comes back. Since he's been booking the band for years now, he and I were always in contact daily, whether he was playing or not. I must say that of all my lifelong friends, Leo knows where most of the bodies are buried.

As a drummer, Leo always brings the perfect amount of punctuation to any song; like Chris, and all the drummers I've ever liked, he never overplays anything; it's always just right in the socket, a groove that makes you dance. When Leo plays, simple, powerful, and clever, it's so right that I forget that he's there.

While his periodic absence caused us some consternation, there was never a thought of giving it up and quitting, and the drummers we got to fill in were the best that our part of the world had to offer though I have to admit, I wondered if fans were starting to get a *Spinal Tap* kind of vibe from the band when new drummers would magically appear with us for a few gigs and then disappear.

For a while our drummer was a guy from central Massachusetts named David Simpaglia. Lags was a heavy metal showman who fit right into the carnival feel of our gigs. We always thought drum solos were funny, and Lags helped us exploit that feeling, because he played them so well.

Then for a few months, Tom Hambridge played with us. Tom was well known in Boston music circles as a guy you could call in a pinch to learn your stuff overnight and jump right in and play, and that's what he did for us. As an example, at that time, when Chuck Berry came to town, he would call Tom and tell him to get a band together.

That's the kind of rep Tom had. I found him

to be every bit the nice guy we'd heard about, and the proud possessor of an excellent sense of humor, which served him well in our employ. Tom didn't know it then, or maybe he did, but he was about to embark on a career that would have him tour with, produce, or write songs for people like Buddy Guy, Meatloaf, Susan Tedeschi, Delbert McClinton, and many others. And let's not forget the three Grammy nominations (which puts him only one behind us) and the many country hits he's written. He also wrote a song for us called 'Henhouse,' a very funny double entendre filled ditty that we still sometimes play.

During another of Leo's absences, we were joined by John Muzzy, but no one calls him that, he's Muzz. Of all the replacement drummers, Muzz was, in many ways, the most perfect fit for us. He'd played in a number of very good Boston bands, but Farrenheit, a band fronted by the great Boston singer/guitar player Charlie Farren, was the band most people then connected him with. Charlie is one of those guys who could sing the phonebook and make it sound good. They opened for Boston on a national tour and had a few hits with 'Lost in Loveland' and 'Fool in Love' that got a lot of MTV play in the late eighties.

Muzz has all the chops of a world class drummer, as well as a flair for hamming it up that puts even me to shame. A few years later, he would hook up with Brad Delp, Joe Holaday, and a knucklehead piano genius named Steve Baker to form the nucleus of the band Beatlejuice, an all Beatles cover band.

The last guy to fill in for Leo was a truly gifted musician named Jim Taft. Jim was with us for a couple of years, and we met no one nicer. The thing about Jim is this; we got him as a drummer, but he probably could have filled in for any of us. He is an amazing singer, he can play guitar, and if you gave him a month, he'd kick ass on bass. Some people are born to play. Also Jim is the only person, whose life I've saved.

I'd like to say that we were taking photos of lions in Zambia when we were attacked by poachers, and that I dragged Jim's half dead body to safety while fending off the attackers, but that's not how it went down. We were in some club west of Boston, and we were eating pizza and doing that hang out after the show thing when Jim came up to me, with a hand on his chest, and a serious look in his eye.

I at first thought he was saying "hi, Mike," but on the off chance that he was saying "Heimlich" I got behind him, wrenched my double fist up into his stomach, and watched a piece of pepperoni fly out of his mouth. There were only about ten people in the room at the time, but they all missed it, showing you once again how close any of us could be to unaided tragedy. Thankfully, Jim survived, and now plays in Danny Klein's Full House, a band started by the J. Geils bass player to honor his personal history and play the tunes his former band mates can't seem to get back together and play.

Sometime in the late nineties, at a band practice, out of the blue Jim said he wanted to quit the band. It's funny that I don't now recall his reasons for giving up the band, but something about the moment made me say "me too." I looked across the room at Rich and Joe and they didn't seem to be arguing.

And just like that, it was over. We made arrangements to go one more time around the New England club circuit as a farewell tour, and said our musical goodbyes to fans and each other. I have a friend who was so upset by our breakup that for years after, he called Jim "Yoko," but it wasn't about him ending the band, it was more that he put something into action that we may have all been thinking.

I knew Rich would find a band and keep playing, and as for me, I'd get to spend more time with Ginny and my daughter Sara. Maybe after thousands of gigs and close to twenty-five years, it was time to put my childish ways behind me and look towards a future without The Fools.

CHAPTER NINETEEN

Time Will Not Erase Us

"The only reason for time is so that everything doesn't happen at once."
Albert Einstein

"If you get up one more time than you fall, you'll make it through."
Proverb

"What do you think this one is?" asked Rich pointing to an item on the menu; we were in Oulu, Finland, about two hours south of the Arctic Circle and we were in a restaurant trying to figure out how to order. We were here on business, working as product demonstrators. The Fools had not played a show in almost two years, and we weren't thinking much about it lately; our current job was taking us all over Europe and America, and it was a complete blast.

"I think this word means moose, but the rest I don't know," I replied, feeling hungry, but completely out of my element. Rich and I were, by now, old hands at ordering in foreign restaurants, but this place had no one who spoke even a smattering of English, and there were no English menus. We both knew enough French, Italian, and Spanish to stay alive in most of the world's restaurants, but who the fuck do you know that can speak Finnish?

Thankfully, there were meals flying by us, carried by the wait staff; food that we could point to. So like three year olds in a candy store, we aimed our fingers at things that went by our table and then pointed to our mouths. Something went by that looked fried and bite sized, so we both excitedly pointed to that and then to our mouths as the waitress took an order to a nearby table. Soon enough a dozen of the fried items, accompanied by a block of some very stinky cheese, were brought to our table by a giggling waitress, and we were chowing the good stuff down.

The name of the restaurant translated to Bear Pot, and we knew that there were not only bear on the menu, but moose, elk, fish, grouse, and something that was probably bobcat. If it locally walked, swam, flew, or crawled, this place had it. At a store we went to, you could even buy a large tin of canned whale meat. In southern New Hampshire, where I now live, I might get accosted for even telling this story but honestly, I understand that these people live in a cold, remote, and highly wooded world, and you do what you must to survive.

Having said that, though we'd only been in town for two days, our opinion of the food was this; they killed it, dragged it inside, cooked it…and without adding much seasoning, they either ate it or served it.

But these fried things were wonderful; kind of like the Ipswich fried clams we grew up with, a little chewy, but crispy on the outside, and creamy on the inside. It was like a taste of home.

We were wondering what to get for our main course; maybe the bear pot stew that the place was known for, when our waitress returned with a much beat up menu. It was in English, and it identified the delightful stuff we were eating; Fried Moose Testicles with Blue Veined Cheese. There are some things that even the best of friends don't discuss; Rich and I don't talk about this.

The reason we were in Finland had to do with us having an actual job and it was no lightweight occupation; we'd been hired by a Massachusetts based company, called MusicPlayground to demonstrate a fantastic new interactive music product. The company had developed a way to take real time signal processing, and translate it into a fun, musical game.

Here's how it worked: you downloaded a CD of information onto your hard drive, and then you'd pay a fee to receive pre-recorded videos of songs (there were hundreds of rock and country hits), then you'd plug one our wired guitar picks, called a V-pic, into your USB port, and play along with the video of whatever song you chose.

When the song video came on your TV or computer screen, you would choose whether to play guitar or bass, and when the song started, you would strike the guitar pick against any hard surface (we chose tennis rackets because they looked guitarish).

As the song played if you hit the pick at the appropriate time, as shown by little lines on the bottom of your screen, and only then would you hear the instrument you were playing as it came up in the song.

You could also hook up a microphone and sing the lead vocal on the song, as the words would scroll on the screen. If this sounds like a precursor to the Guitar Hero game, that's exactly what it was. While it was marketed as a kind of karaoke game on steroids, the real fun was being able to play lead guitar on songs like 'Bad to the Bone.' The MusicPlayground cover of that George Thorogood & The Destroyers hit contained a perfect copy of the solo-but only if you used the V-pic correctly.

People's eyes constantly lit up when they realized that if they hit the pic at the right time, they were "playing the guitar."

So now it was the late nineties, and Rich and I were once again seeing the world, but this time as product demonstrators for this wonderful game.

The company sent us to Finland to the annual ridiculously delightful Air Guitar World Championships. It's just what it sounds like: contestants from all over the world descend on Oulu, Finland, and get up onstage in front of thousands to acrobatically play make believe guitars to their favorite songs.

I think the year that we were there, someone

from Australia won, but anyhow, it seemed a perfect place for us to demo our terrific toy. We got up on the stage in front of the large crowd, and with a huge TV screen behind us, showed people that anyone, with a little practice, could use our V-pic and seem to play guitar.

Rich and I in London with an appropriate sign

The audience loved it, and soon we had people lining up to try it. We weren't surprised, this reaction happened everywhere we went; whether it was in France, Germany, or at one of our many demos at trade shows or clubs throughout North America. And because Rich and I did our jobs well, we were told that when the company hit, we would be well taken care of. We weren't the only ones in the company who thought it could happen, and it seemed like only a matter of time before the world caught on to our product.

In 2001 we even brought our toy to the private, post premiere party of the film *Rock Star*, held at the House of Blues in Los Angeles. Although the movie was pretty crappy, it wasn't because of Mark Wahlberg, a South Boston boy, and one of my favorite actors. He had no problem playing a rock star, because of course he had been one.

Jennifer Aniston, still with Brad Pitt, played the girlfriend and she was also quite fine in the movie. She and Pitt both showed up at the party, and some people were heard to say, "damn, she looks perfect and so does he." Like most Americans, I had strong hopes that their relationship would stand the test of time, and that we would be talking about Brad and Jen intertwined for years to come…and I was truly heartbroken when their tryst ended….okay, I'm just fucking with you, I don't care what they do, it's their business, and if either one of them in their private lives wants to marry a fucking turtle, I will still look at their work and say it was very good.

I know this falls into the category of "Mike-no one wants to hear your stupid movie reviews" but damn, there have been so many bad rock films. I won't list them, but the movie Rock Star was just another poor take on the rock business, which has had only a few movies that have properly depicted it. I'm not going to list the good ones either, but ironically enough, Rob Reiner's great satirical movie *This is Spinal Tap* is probably the closest depiction of what long term band life is like, complete with inter-band politics, exploding drummers, and the crazy band girlfriend who thinks her connection to her guy should make everyone else take her band related ideas seriously. There is also the shrinking audience syndrome, spoken of in the film as an audience becoming "more selective."

As our luck would have it, the MusicPlayground thing did not catch on, in spite of the best work of its visionary founder, and nice guy, Brad Naples, and the help of another old friend and rock lawyer powerhouse Frank Cimler, the dude who brought me and Rich onboard. Frank has had dealings with some of the biggest bands on the planet; Aerosmith and The Rolling Stones to name a couple, but in the end none of this mattered to the world.

Maybe it had to do with the fact that our company wanted inroads into your hard drive (yipes!), or that we expected monthly payments from you, (yipes! again) or that our magic was located in a guitar pick and not some cheap plastic guitar replication. The short story is this; the company went under.

What you see now as *Guitar Hero* is essentially what we were trying to sell people, but their use of our technology, and their better understanding of what people will pay illustrates this point: it doesn't matter about the historical argument as to who made the first light bulb…Thomas Edison produced the one that made the big cash.

During this two year time period, other than occasionally sitting in with a fun cover band called Drive In, that included my still friends for life, the Pedrick Brothers, I wasn't playing in a band. But Rich Bartlett was, and so was Joe Holaday. They both ended up playing with what they thought of as old friends, but what the world sees as rock icons; Rich with Ben Orr, and Joe with Brad Delp. Ben was out playing Cars' tunes in a band called ORR and needed a guitar player who could perfectly play his stuff; so he called Rich. Joe, in 1994, along with Brad Delp, and three very gifted musicians, Bob Squires, Steve Baker, and old friend Muzz, was a founding member of Beatlejuice, a band that as Brad used to say, played "all Beatles, all night." Until we broke up in the late nineties, Joe played in both The Fools and Beatlejuice, which was a juggling act to book, but it all worked out. Beatlejuice also became Brad's home away from Boston, and Joe's home away from The Fools. Dave Mitchell, an excellent and versatile guitarist, eventually replaced Bob Squires and that was the Beatlejuice lineup for years after.

As the new century kicked in, and our time with MusicPlayground was winding down, we got a get-back-together offer that was impossible to refuse. The offers to play had never really stopped coming in, and they were mostly from clubs, some as large as the 1,800 seat Hampton Beach Casino, some as small as the 200 hundred seat C-Note in Hull.

We said the same thing to all of them: no. But in one case, a very nice, pretty, and apparently wealthy young woman from Southern New Hampshire contacted us about playing a New Year's Eve party at her home. She'd seen us a few years before, and thought we would be the perfect complement to a night that already included a hundred guests, high end catering and big time fireworks. We said no.

She thought we were being coy (we weren't) and so she raised the already high price. We said no again. She must have decided that this was a game she was going to win, because only an idiot would have turned down her next offer. We didn't. We may be Fools, but we're not idiots.

Rich, Joe, Leo, and I had a few rehearsals, although we probably only needed to write a set list… our years together had created great muscle memory that was very easy to click back into.

We played the show, it went well, and we knew instantly after that, we had to put the band back together. We did, and I'm proud to say The Fools have been together ever since, with only one change. Because of Joe's now almost constant work with Beatlejuice, we eventually had to make the choice to replace him.

This time, for once, we didn't do auditions, although like people with no memory for pain, we were tempted. A friend of ours, Jeff Matte, suggested a guy named Lou Spagnola he'd seen in an excellent New England based eighties cover band called Fortune. We met Lou, he played everything perfectly, and he's been our guy ever since.

Lou is not only a bass player of style, power, and talent, but also a Boston sports fan that puts even my extensive sports knowledge to shame. With no time for thought, Lou can tell you who was playing second base for the Sox when the ball went through Buckner's legs in '86. I've thought more than once that we could possibly lose Lou down the line to a sports talk show.

That pretty much brings us up to the near present. We put out a CD of all new material called *10* back in 2008 that ironically was probably the more serious album that Peter wanted us to make in the eighties. Not that it's full of funeral dirges, but there are a lot more reflective and thoughtful tunes like 'Time Will Not Erase Us' and 'Million Miles' than we'd ever have considered doing thirty years ago.

The Fools today

We're also playing more gigs today than we have in years, most nights to a packed house. Maybe it's because we've lasted so long, but we've come back into vogue with the people who go out to see bands. They say things like, "I can't believe you guys are still together" but it's a compliment and not an insult. More than one person lately has shown up with not only a son or daughter, but a grandson or granddaughter, and said something like, "I wanted them to see you guys before you stop playing." I don't think that's going to happen any time soon, but who knows?

There are so many things that can break up a band; illness, jealousy, family things, money, love, hate, death, and ambition to name a few. There were nights when I knew I couldn't go on stage, but I did. I played the night after my Mom died. I played only two days after rupturing my Achilles tendon, and was carried onstage. I played just days after my Dad died.

It wasn't about me being a stone cold motherfucker; it was about me doing all I could for my much loved biological family, and then escaping into the healing love of music with my musical family. The guy I am on stage is careless, confident, flippant, and ready for anything; if I climb out on a musical limb, and the band carves it off, I'm fine with that. It's all about the created experience.

The thing that has saved me so often, from bad days, dark moods, and the occasional horrible shrapnel that life sends your way, has been the knowledge that I would have to get on stage that night and lay down that knapsack full of rocks down.

I never felt it was fair to the audience to bring your temporary darkness or bad life situation to the stage, but saying that makes me sound a little too happy ass and altruistic. It's been more of a two way street, I could have an absolutely horrible day and that night, I knew I could escape into the great shake, rattle, and roll of what playing music for people gives you.

EPILOGUE

Early on into this century, we brought Stacey back into the band. It was like he never left.

There is now a street in Ipswich named Foolish Avenue. It's a short but happy street.

Doug Forman sometimes gets up and plays a tune or two with us, as does Chris, but his main work, running the numbers of the Pedrick mining empire, takes up most of his time. Thankfully, I still haven't been in Pedrick's hole.

I haven't had much contact with Peter, but I think he's still working out of New York, maybe looking for that next big thing. He's a talented man and I wish him well.

Brad Delp took his life in '07. It was a personal choice, but it left many people utterly devastated. Brad was so friendly to so many, that you had the feeling you knew him. As it turned out, I guess almost no one really did. I'd been friends with him since around the time Boston started, and even after they'd achieved mega status, he would sometimes

Brad presents us with an award at the 1989 Boston Music Awards

come to Fools' gigs, at some club somewhere, and hang around till the end of the night, when you'd see him helping the road crew wrap up cords.

We never told anyone who he was, and anyhow,

who would have believed that the lead singer of the biggest band on the planet was helping us load out. I'll say now what so many others have said before, Brad was a sweet guy but sometimes it's hard to balance that with how desperately and violently he ended his place in this world.

To celebrate his life, Muzz arranged a three day tribute at The Regent Theater in Arlington that was both deeply moving and very entertaining. I sang at it, as did many other Brad fans. Not long after the tribute, the main players in the band, Joe, Muzz, Steve, and Dave, decided that they didn't want the Beatlejuice thing to end, and recruited singers like me, Jimmy Rogers, Buddy Bernard, and Bob Jennings to try and keep it going. I do it when it doesn't conflict with a Fools' show as does Rich, and it's great fun to play those wonderful songs with such a good group of talented and funny people.

That was almost four years ago, and it's still rolling along; all Beatles, all night.

On August 12, 2009 WBCN went silent. What was the spokesman of Boston rock for forty years and the station that had stood by The Fools since the beginning was suddenly gone. The final fitting words broadcast over the air were those of the late "Cosmic Muffin" Darrell Martini, "over and out."

Later that month we were asked to play a final show in celebration of the station at The Paradise, a Boston club we'd done live radio broadcasts from for 'BCN in the late seventies and early eighties. It was great to see Charles, Carter, Oedipus and many of the other good people who helped to give us our start. It was also a solemn reminder that all good things do indeed come to an end.

I didn't see Gino again until we met by chance in an Ipswich bar in the early nineties. He knew by my look that I was crushed to see him; I felt like I'd betrayed him all those years ago. He looked hard at me and said, "I can't believe you had the fucking balls to fire me." Then he laughed and bought me a beer, and we talked band "war stories" for a while until it felt like we could be friends again…and soon we were. He was still working security at the nuclear plant, still with Debby, and now they'd added a young daughter. He seemed to be happy.

I didn't see him often after that, but one meeting stands out; I was in a supermarket with my then two year old daughter Sara who was sitting in the seat of a shopping cart, when we turned a corner and there he was. I introduced the big man to my tiny daughter and he instantly became a harmless clown for her benefit. She thought he was fantastic, and he was. Gino always said "play the room," and that's what he was doing.

I got a call from a friend not long after that telling me that right after taking a medical stress test, that he had passed, Gino dropped dead. I was stunned; he always seemed indestructible to me.

Some people, you choose to remember them how you want. Gino was the palace guard, an honest to God tough guy but through all the years I knew him, I never saw him abuse his power. In our rock n' roll world, he was the go to guy for anything important, and he could always be trusted to keep a confidence. I like to think that he would have enjoyed this book, and laughed hard at some of the tales involving him. I don't just speak for me when I say, he always seemed larger than life.

Well, that's it, that's how it was, or at least as well as I can remember it. Hopefully there are more foolish tales to be told and more songs to be sung, but I should stop now; I've got a gig tonight.

BONUS STUFF

Long before the age of the internet, we passed out newsletters at our shows to do roughly what's done on the net today; advertising our upcoming shows, provide info about the band, etc. These have been unseen since the early days of the band in the late seventies. Enjoy!

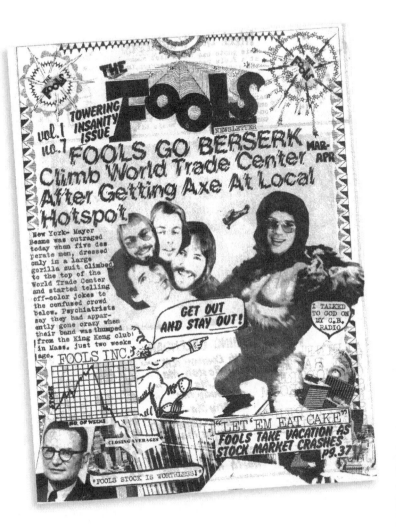

THE FOOLS DISCOGRAPHY

Sold Out
Original Release Date: 1980
EMI Records
1. Night Out
2. Fine With Me
3. Sold Out
4. Sad Story
5. Mutual of Omaha
6. It's a Night for Beautiful Girls
7. Spent the Rent
8. Easy for You
9. I Won't Grow Up

**First Annual Official Unofficial
Fools Day**
Original Release 1980
EMI Records
Introduction
1. Spent The Rent
2. Night Out
3. It's A Night For Beautiful Girls
4. Don't Tell Me
5. I Won't Grow Up
6. Psycho Chicken

Heavy Mental
Original Release Date: 1981
EMI Records
1. Mind Control
2. Dressed in White
3. Around the Block
4. Local Talent
5. Lost Number
6. What I Tell Myself
7. Last Cadillac on Earth
8. Coming Home With Me
9. Running Scared
10. Tell Me You Love Me
11. Alibi

World Dance Party
Original Release Date: 1985
(re-released 2003)
Ouch Records
1. *I Love Your Tits*
2. *Bigfoot Stole My Wife*
3. *Doo Wah Diddy*
4. *Untouchables*
5. *Mr. Big*
6. *It's A Night*
7. *Life Sucks...Then You Die*
8. *World Dance Party*
9. *Sex*
10. *I Rock, Therefore I Am*
11. *Can't Keep My Mind On You*
12. *She Makes Me Feel Big*
13. *Long And Hard*
14. *Back To The Real World*

Wake Up...It's Alive!!!
Original Release Date: 1988
Ouch Records
1. *When the Lights Go Out*
2. *I Love Money*
3. *World Dance Party*
4. *Bite It!*
5. *The Blooze*
6. *Can You Dance to It*
7. *The Sound of Silence*
8. *What I'd Do for You*
9. *Mack the Knife*
10. *That's It, Go Home*

Rated XXX
Original Release Date: 1990
Ouch Records
1. *Oh Betty*
2. *Texas Chainsaw Square Dance Massacre*
3. *I Love Pigs*
4. *Too Many Ways to Die (Country)*
5. *Tom Dooley*
6. *I'm Drunk*
7. *Life Sucks...Then You Die*
8. *Play With Me*
9. *L.L. Cool Bean*
10. *I'm a Nun*
11. *Bite It*
12. *Let's Go to Bed*
13. *She Makes Me Feel Big*
14. *Too Many Ways to Die (City)*
15. *Kill for the Devil*

Show Em' Your Nuts
Original Release Date: 1991
Ouch Records
1. *Plumbing On My Mind*
2. *Hen House*
3. *Love Pajamas*
4. *Rookie At The Plate*
5. *Sports And Beer*
6. *Scary Movies*
7. *Drop A Dime*
8. *Phantom Of The Laundromat*
9. *I Feel Good Tonight*
10. *Grandma*
11. *I Don't Know*
12. *Kinky*

Christmas Toons
Original Release Date: 1992
Ouch Records
1. *I Shot Santa in my Underwear*
2. *X-Mas With a Bottle and a Jukebox*
3. *Christmas Loser*
4. *Norburt the Nearsighted Reindeer*
5. *Christmas Stress*
6. *King of Christmas*
7. *A Christmas Story*
8. *Rockin Rollin Over Christmas*
9. *Santa Bird-Dogged my Baby*
10. *My Dog Died on Christmas Day*
11. *Rockin in a Christmas / New Year*

Coors Light Sixpack
Original Release Date: 2000
Released by Ouch Records
1. Psycho Chicken
2. Spent the Rent
3. Night Out
4. The Truth
5. Won't Grow Up
6. Alibi

The F in Beach Album
Original Release Date: 2003
Released by Ouch Records
1. Introduction
2. More Of Everything
3. Psycho Chicken
4. Night Out
5. Can't Keep My Mind on You
6. World Dance Party
7. Bite It
8. Just Give Up
9. Things That Lovers Do
10. Brain
11. It's a Night (For Beautiful Girls)
12. Life Sucks...Then You Die!!!
13. I Won't Grow Up
14. Gun on my Radio
15. She Makes Me Feel Big
16. That's It, Go Home

10
Original Release Date: 2007
Released by Ouch Records
1. Time Will Not Erase Us
2. Dancin' on the Moon
3. No Free Love
4. Last Time
5. Time Goes Slipping By
6. Be All Right
7. Fever Dream
8. Fly with Me
9. All I Got
10. Million Miles

European only release – cover of
The Nervous Eater's 'Talk to Loretta'

World Dance Party VHS Release

ABOUT THE AUTHOR

Mike really did grow up in Ipswich, MA, really did tour the world as a member of the rock band The Fools and really does have a wife named Ginny and daughter they named Sara. Everything else in-between is pretty much open to your interpretation of the events.

Mike enjoys playing video games, is an enthusiastic reader, collects underground comic books and loves to play with his daughter's German Shepherd Stella.

Also from Sons of Liberty Publishing

Two Redheads & A Dead Blonde
A Ronan Marino Mystery

By Lloyd L. Corricelli

Ronan Marino thought his life was going to be easy when he won lottery, left a successful career in the military and moved back to his boyhood home in Lowell, Massachusetts....he couldn't have been more wrong. When his girlfriend is found dead in the cold waters of the Merrimack River, Ronan learns she had a dark secret; one that powerful men on both sides of the law are desperate to remain hidden. Calling on his mob enforcer cousin for backup, Ronan dives headfirst into places where even angels fear to tread; committed to finding who took his girlfriend's life even at the cost of his own.

Thunder From Rain

By Eugene Sockut

For one hundred and thirteen days in 1877, a strange, savage and tragically bloody Indian war was fought across 1,400 miles of nearly impassible terrain in Oregon, Idaho, and Montana as 600 Nez Perce Indians endeavored to fight their way through the American Army of the Northwest to freedom in Canada. Thunder From Rain is the painfully true story of how the benevolent Nez Perce Indians, who had saved the explorers Lewis and Clark in 1805, were forcibly and against their will transformed into one of the most formidable foes the U.S. Army ever faced. Told through the eyes of a young cavalry officer who served under the generals in charge of the pursuit, this tale is replete with the historical intrigues, corruption and selfish ambitions of the time.

Whisper of the Seventh Thunder

By USA Today Bestselling
author Larry Brooks

Author of Darkness Bound,
Pressure Points & Bait & Switch

Winner - Best Suspense/Thriller Novel

2010 Next Generation Indie Book Award

When Gabriel Stone's devout wife dies in an unlikely airline disaster, he finishes the novel she had warned him not to write. The book goes inside and behind the Bible's Book of Revelation to reveal startling connections to covert operations that are, quite unknown to Stone, about to tear the world's political landscape to shreds. As the book nears publication Stone suddenly finds himself the pawn in a war between superpowers and supernatural forces, each with hidden agendas beyond his comprehension and stakes that pivot on his ability to accept the unbelievable and stop the unthinkable. "Whisper of the Seventh Thunder" is a book that is as personal as it is global in scope, juxtaposing choices that are at once spiritual and life-dependant, with nothing short of our very souls hanging in the balance.

Coffin Dust

By David Daniel

Author of Reunion, The Marble Kite and White Rabbit

In the vein of Richard Matheson's Shock collections and Stephen King's Night Shift, Coffin Dust culls twenty plus of David Daniel's short stories from the magazines where they first appeared. Varied in style and tone, these tales all possess, in the words of the late Theodore Sturgeon, "a touch of the strange." Moody, atmospheric, and sharply drawn, they present ordinary people who find themselves drawn into odd little corners of life.

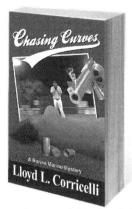

Chasing Curves
A Ronan Marino Mystery

By Lloyd L. Corricelli

Private detective Ronan Marino returns with an all new mystery. When college pitching phenom Ty Wallace is accused of murdering his prospective agent's secretary, the ballplayer's father enlists Ronan Marino to clear his son and uncover the real killer. Working the hardscrabble streets of Lowell and the upscale Boston Back Bay neighborhood, Ronan uncovers a series of clues leading him right into a web of blackmail, gambling and sex; a conspiracy seemingly directed by his boyhood idol, a former Red Sox player and his partner in crime, a renegade gangster aiming to wrestle control of the Boston family from Ronan's uncle. With his mobster cousin Tony and Lowell Police detective Eddie Garcia providing backup, "the best that money can't buy" once again finds himself caught between the light and darkness; desperate to solve the murder and figure out why his personal life continues to be such a mess.

Coming Soon

Spy in the City Of Books
By Stephen O'Connor

Take the Long Way Home
By J.F. Dacey

Mill City Stories
By David Daniel, Lloyd L. Corricelli and others

The Vicious Circle
A Ronan Marino Mystery
By Lloyd L. Corricelli

Please visit our website at:

www.SonsofLibertyPublishing.com

Sons of Liberty
Publishing

Made in the USA
Middletown, DE
23 February 2019